HOPE IS A VERB

MY JOURNEY OF IMPOSSIBLE TRANSFORMATION

Amy Downs

DEDICATION

I dedicate this book to two spouses. One is mine, Terry Head, and one is the wife of my nephew, Caleb McCoy, who was my ghostwriter and collaborator behind this book.

Courtney McCoy, without your support this book would not have been possible. Thank you for encouraging and supporting Caleb to share this message of hope and living as a book widow for a year.

Terry, you model servant leadership for me. You are my rock, cycling buddy, lover, and best friend. You are my everything. Thank you for always guiding and pointing me toward Christ.

TABLE OF CONTENTS

Part One

SURVIVOR

2017 Ironman Arizona

Hour Zero

THE RED LIGHT blinked on the smoke detector on my hotel room ceiling. It was three in the morning and there was no way I'd sleep any longer. The sheet caught the rough skin at the corners of my toes as I took a silent roll call of my muscles, asking them to announce their strength. I'd need everything they could give me to complete an Ironman triathlon in the desert of Tempe, Arizona. That meant, in a single day, swimming 2.4 miles, cycling for 112 miles, and finishing the day with, you know, a light marathon run of 26.2 miles. Over the past few weeks, I'd eaten a mountain of pasta and guzzled gallons of sports drinks to build up a hyper-hydrated concoction of ready-to-burn calories. And yet, my thighs and calves felt normal. Uninspired. They were like the red light blinking on the ceiling. Calm, steady, and muted. I wondered if that meant they were fully charged, or empty.

AC/DC erupted from my phone's alarm with the *Thunder* chorus. I burrowed my face into my husband's mustache and let the guitar and Brian Johnson squeal.

"It's today," I whispered in his ear.

"Can you call it day yet?" he groaned but kissed my forehead. I used the restroom and slicked body glide on my thighs, underarms, and all over my chest. I crammed into my Venganza tri kit, a matching set of skintight, sweat-wicking, and water-resistant spandex shorts and top cut off at my shoulders. It was pink and black with three yellow streaks like a claw gouging my heart. The tight fit squeezed cellulite-pitted chunks of skin above my knee, but the black fabric made an outline of my muscles packed underneath. Of all the ways my body had looked over the years, this was my favorite. Cellulite and all.

I put on a wind jacket and slipped into pink flip-flops. "All set," I said. There was no makeup to apply or hair to manage. I'd trained for over a year for this day. In some ways, I'd been training my whole life. And now that it was here, it had taken me seven minutes to get ready.

"Did you pack your sandwiches?" Terry said through his toothbrush, clearly not impressed with my world record time.

I opened the hotel mini-fridge and threw some frozen, foil-wrapped Uncrustables into the five white bags scattered across the floor. They each had the number 1798 written on every side. Terry strapped the official Ironman time chip to my ankle and we hauled the five bags into the cool, dry air of the early morning desert.

"My running shoes!" I said as I slapped the dashboard.

"In the third bag," Terry pointed to the backseat.

"Turn around, I left the pickle juice."

"First bag."

We parked and carried my bags into the transition area with thousands of athletes and volunteers buzzing in the dark. Headlamps flashed in the teeming crowd of bright yellow, lavender, and tangerine outfits with sporadic chatters of nervous laughter breaking across the lawn. We dropped my bags off at the official check-in, and a volunteer with half of her hair chopped to her skull marked the number *1798* with a thick black marker on my arm and calf.

We weaved through elevated metal racks of bicycles hung by their seats. Even with the crowd and the dark, my bike was easy to find. It had a bright pink frame because, in case you aren't following along, my life is pink. I loaded some frozen water bottles on the frame and did a double-check in my transition bag for my cycling socks, shoes, gloves, jacket, sunglasses, and helmet. Then I did a triple-check, quadruple-check, and whatever-comes-after-quadruple-check.

"The Wal-Mart sacks!" I yelled.

"Lilly Ann," Terry said, using my middle name as he held up two Wal-Mart plastic sacks. I kissed him and leaned against a bench to start the slow battle of my will against the best modern engineering of the twenty-first century. My wetsuit was made of a hybrid rubber called neoprene designed to suction water-tight to my skin, which made it darn-near impossible to slide your skin into the thing. I wrapped a Wal-Mart bag around each foot and slid through the leg holes before the neoprene stuck to my legs. Then I wiggled and hopped on one foot that probably looked like Tom Cruise's tighty-whitey dance in *Risky Business* to force the rest of the suit up my legs. By the time I had the wetsuit over my rump, my forehead was moist with sweat and my legs felt raw from the friction. Then I had to get my arms through, which took some substantial help from Terry and my Oklahoma training buddies stretching the back of my suit in the same way a puppy is picked up by the skin of her neck.

"Is this really happening?" I asked once we'd all recovered from zipping into our wetsuits. I trained a full year with Chris, Ruth, and Linda. We'd grown close over the many, many, many miles of swims, rides, and runs. They looked at me, each one trying to give me a response, but no one had a good answer. "Why did we sign up for this?" I asked. No one had an answer for that, either.

The sky turned gray and the lake came into focus. It looked more like a long, still river with bridges spanning a quarter-mile shore to shore, one with holiday lights strewn across its arching ropes. We could spot the veteran and elite athletes. They were shouldering through the crowd with calm faces to jockey a position closer to the lake. They moved naturally in their tight wetsuits and neon green and pink head caps, as if wearing pajamas. One group jogged around the street because, apparently, today's race wasn't already long enough. We took tiny shuffles toward the back of the three thousand athletes. A girl with pink hair next to us was crying. I heard the distinctive retching sound of someone losing their breakfast. I checked my Garmin smartwatch. It said the wind should be calm today, so that was good. I mean, a calm wind made the impossible distance easier, right? Right?

A guy behind us still had his wetsuit unzipped to his waist. He was hairless with something like a seven or eleven pack of abs. "Aren't you supposed to be up there?" I asked the guy, pointing up the line. We were supposed to line up according to our expected swim time, with the fastest in front and the slowest at the back. There was no reason for a Michael Phelps clone with zero body fat to be anywhere near a large-frame Athena like me.

"The swim part scares me," he said, smiling with perfect white teeth.

An announcer boomed from the speakers. We all knew his voice. It was Mike Reilly, or as I knew him, the Voice of Ironman. If you Google almost any video of an Ironman race, you'll hear his call in the tone of rock and fire, each word communicating both stone-steady assurance and a burning furnace of encouragement to push harder. If ever a man sounded like the voice of God, it was Mike Reilly. And it was every athlete's dream to hear his voice call their name at the finish line, declaring their new title of Ironman to the universe.

I grabbed Ruth's hand. "Is it too late to back out?" I asked. The same thought seemed to flash in her eyes. There was no way we'd finish the day. We were fools to think our aging, back-of-the-pack bodies could accomplish the impossible distance reserved for the actual athletes bouncing around us.

We can do this, I tried to reassure myself. *All things are possible when you have hope.*

An actual cannon blasted, echoing across the lake and in my chest. For a moment, the world spun in my mind and Ruth held my hand until I'd calmed down. The elite athletes splashed in the lake in a wave of white foam. I looked at Terry in the crowd. As if he could hear my own thoughts, he mouthed to me, "You've got hope."

Then we waited. It took at least fifteen minutes after the cannon blast for us to make the final descent to the lake, which felt like a fifteen-minute climb up the first hill on a roller coaster. Every passing second was like another loud metallic clack telling you the drop on the other side just got a little bit higher and scarier but, sorry, you're already strapped in and can't escape. There was nothing to do but slowly tiptoe toward the lake and pretend to be excited.

I added my pink flip-flops to the piles of littered sandals down the gated path. My bare feet felt lukewarm moisture seeping through the mat. "Why is it so wet?" I asked. Chris pointed to a tiny stream in the concrete next to the ramp, trickling down into the lake.

"Let me put it this way," the Michael Phelps clone behind us laughed. He had finally zipped up his wetsuit and looked like a superhero with huge shoulders teetering on a tiny waist. "It's not water."

It took me a moment to realize what he meant. The athletes had waited in line so long this morning, with so much coffee and adrenaline pumping, they couldn't hold it until they got into the water. And once you were in a wetsuit there was no getting out, so a quick restroom run wasn't an option. Instead, three thousand athletes had been peeing in their suits all morning, creating a full stream flowing into the lake.

"Go, go, go!" the volunteers yelled. The four of us Okies squeezed our hands in a brief circle. I tried to memorize the moment. It was seven in the morning in the Tempe desert. To the east, the sky had ignited behind the distant purple mountains with the colors of red roses and honey. The hues reflected on the lake like rippling gold.

Gold, like the color of urine streaming into the lake.

"His mercies are new every morning," I muttered as I pressed start on my Garmin watch, jumped into the cold water, and took my first strokes toward the fire on the horizon.

Chapter One

False Hope

"WHY WOULD YOU move to Oklahoma City?"

The question's strange wording caught me off guard. I was sitting in a conference room at the Federal Employees Credit Union in October of 1988. Kathy Finley, a blonde professional with sparkling earrings dangling down her long, elegant neck, was interviewing me for an entry-level teller position. I'd been prepared to answer questions like "*What* brought you here?" or "Why *did* you move?" But this beautiful model of a businesswoman had asked me why *would* I move here, which sounded like an accusation. Like I was some kind of crazy to voluntarily move to Oklahoma City. I hesitated for a few awkward seconds while a hundred thoughts raced through my mind. I didn't know it at the time, but I was about to answer her question with the most damaging lie of my life.

IT WOULD HAVE taken my life story to fully answer Kathy's question. I was born in Shreveport, Louisiana as the youngest of five kids when my mom was forty years old. That wasn't common in 1967 and was certainly not planned by my parents, a fact that was always clear to me. My birth was like the final detail painted into the background of a

Norman Rockwell family portrait. A pleasing addition, but the painting was perfect before. My closest sister, Donna, was ten years older than me. My closest brother, Alan, was five years older. My first memories of my oldest brother, Mike, was when he came home to visit from college and would twirl me with ease in his arms.

Before I started school, I'd roam the empty house and swing on the back porch by myself. I believed my parents when they said Jesus was always with me, so I'd scoot over on the swing for Jesus to sit beside me and leave space on my pillow at night for Jesus to rest his head. When my sisters were home, they took time to play house or dolls with me, but they were too old to drop into my level of pretend fantasies. By the time I started kindergarten, they were wearing makeup and driving cars. Donna was one of my first Sunday school teachers, using puppets behind a curtain to sing "Can't Nobody Do Me Like Jesus" by Andraé Crouch and the Disciples. If anything, my sisters were more like aunts helping raise me, which left a big, open space in my heart where I needed a friend.

When I started school, we moved to a house in the country with twelve acres, a barn, and two horses. It was a beautiful property shrouded with longleaf pine trees, which are unique to the Shreveport area. Rather than normal, stout pine trees like a Christmas tree, these trees had tall, pale trunks that rose two stories before the first branches arched out. I often thought their tips were magic pens dotting the billions of stars in the country night sky.

The rest of my family loved getting away from the city. For me, the country meant fewer playdates and walking alone in an even wider emptiness. The only sound that broke the terrible silence was my scream when a bug scuttled beneath my shoe or a cricket jumped across my shin.

I exchanged my best friend Jesus for Bobo, a stray dog we adopted one Saturday after he dropped a half-decomposed cow skull on our back porch. We'd originally called him Hobo because of the leaves tangled in his patchy fur, but we all agreed on Bobo the Circus Dog when my brother Alan discovered he could do a full backflip on demand. Whenever we pulled down into our long driveway, our gray-haired horse Freddy would run down the fence of his pen and Bobo would jump, bite, and clench Freddy's tail in his jaws, swinging like a pendulum behind Freddy's rump. Bobo protected me from the nasty bugs during my long afternoons and weekends alone. I explained to him the flowers in my mom's garden were pretty because God wanted to make us happy and reminded him to ask Jesus into his heart so I would have a friend in heaven.

In high school, my dad gave me a white diesel Ford Ranger pickup and I was finally free from the prison of the woods. I imagined the puff of black smoke that popped when the truck started was like the disciples dusting off their feet from an unwelcome town. I found a real best friend with a girl named Mary and we started a drama club at church. Soon, we were asked to perform at other churches across the city. We had little skits based on *Mama's Family* with our hair curled high on our heads. I learned to mimic Carol Burnett's best anguished and ticked-off faces, ending every skit with my best "Mammaa!"

I also got serious with a boy. Seth was the drummer in a Christian rock band called Advocate, which was pretty daring for the time. Back then, a lot of Christians thought it was offensive for anyone to indulge in a sinful guitar or, even worse, drum solo. The genre that had swooning women tossing their bras onto the stage didn't belong in a church. Being Seth's number-one fan made me feel part of the rebel rock attitude. I loved helping set up and break down his drum sets for shows around the city. From the way I acted, you'd have thought Advocate had airtime on the radio and sold-out concert venues. The reality was their biggest show was at the local skating rink with maybe fifty kids, and the rest of the performances were on Wednesday nights for the few dozen in youth groups. When we graduated, Seth gave me a promise ring, which was a kind of third-degree commitment people did back then—a promise to one day get on a knee to promise to, one day, promise to love me forever. We started college and I felt my future was as bright as the sun's reflection off that promise ring.

As it turned out, my future was precisely as promising as that thin ring. I flunked out of both semesters my first year in college, failing remedial math twice. The only class I managed to pass was Speech, so at least I was still qualified to talk. Seth struggled, too, and ended up joining the military. He came back from basic training a little different. It was nothing terrible or dark, but he wasn't the same carefree drummer of Advocate. The soul of rock music was about upheaving the system, not becoming part of the big, bureaucratic government machine. I'd grown up listening to my dad's tales of World War II and the life of a military wife didn't appeal to me. Pretty soon after his return, we broke up.

When I was a kid, the only non-Christian television program I'd been allowed to watch was *The Lawrence Welk Show*, a variety show with a big band with trumpets, beautiful dresses, and dancing. The earlier shows were sponsored by Geritol, a liquid supplement tonic with iron. Every show started with an image of the Geritol bottle and a shot of floating bubbles as the intro credits scrolled. My dad would lean over the couch and say, "Hey, brat girl, that's the job you'll have one day. You're going to be the bubble blower."

After failing college, my dad tried to smooth over his jovial comments, "Why go to college?" he'd say. "You're pretty. You'll get married." But I wasn't getting married now. There was no engagement ring or even a promise ring on my finger. No one took me out on a date. I was twenty-one years old with no degree, living in my parents' house. Both of them were over sixty years old and would go to bed early, leaving me alone to sit in the sun room at the back of the house. Only at night, there was no sun to fill the room with warmth. Instead, the cold, brick floor sucked the heat out of my bare feet as I stared out the massive bay windows into the swaying trees bathed in the moon's cobalt light. I imagined a distant darkness swallowing the trees in the back of our property and was terrified the void would swallow me next.

So, I THOUGHT after Kathy asked her question at my interview, *why would I move to Oklahoma City?* I couldn't tell her my life story, but there were lots of shorter answers I could give her.

I had a broken heart.

I was desperately lonely.

I was barely eating or sleeping.

I finally managed to blurt out, "I have a sister who lives here."

"Oh, okay," she said in a slightly higher octave, indicating I hadn't explained anything by that statement. I started to joke about living in Donna's cramped house of five boys, but then I would have to admit I was sleeping on the floor in a baby room next to her infant son. There was no way this gorgeous, sophisticated businesswoman would hire me if I mentioned how much perfume it took to mask the poopy-diaper smell that permeated everything in the room where I slept.

"I really like Oklahoma City," I added. Which was kind of true but also not. So far, my experiences downtown had been foreboding. A few days earlier, I'd had a creepy interview in an abandoned warehouse with a man promising to make me a branch manager in his credit union while his knee brushed mine. Earlier that morning, my car door made an ugly clanking sound as a mighty gust almost tore it off the hinges. I had to flag down some passing businessmen to help me close the door again, keeping one hand bunched around my skirt to keep from flashing all of downtown.

"I'm just hoping for a new life here, you know," I added quickly.

That was it. Without knowing it, I told Kathy the biggest lie of my life. And that lie was going to hurt me. A lot.

YOU SEE, I thought I knew what the word *hope* meant. I grew up in a conservative Christian family. We talked about hope all the time. *Jesus is the hope of the nations,* we'd sing at church. Every time hope came up in the scriptures, I thought about a brighter future. In the future, somewhere, there would be hope. If anything, hope was like a prayer. If you wanted something to change, you prayed about it and quoted the Bible. It was a kind of wish. Outside the church, people often think the same way. Headed to the airport, someone might say, "I hope you have a good flight." Or when month-end reports are being prepared, someone might say "I hope we did well." You could replace *hope* with the word *wish* in almost every instance the word is used.

But that's not what *hope* means. There is so much more to that beautiful word than some distant desire on the horizon, but its true meaning has been lost. Or, at least, it was lost to me. It was like I'd misplaced its raw power with something simple and quaint. It was like mistaking a lightning bolt for a flashlight. Or the North Atlantic Current for a quiet woodland stream. I'd diminished the power of hope by using its name to describe small, helpless things. I'd crippled hope into a mere wish.

I didn't understand any of this in '88. Instead, to me, hope was some destination on the horizon. As I sat in Shreveport rocking in the dark night, I wished for a better future. I wished my broken heart would heal. I wished a man would rescue and marry me. I wished a new job would fulfill me. I wished God would snap his fingers and make everything better again. I thought of the lullaby my mom used to sing:

Surely goodness and mercy will follow Amy
All the days of her life

As a child, I actually believed those were the exact words of the scripture. As if the pages of the Bible were written and preserved for millennia with the name Amy etched inside for me and me alone. Staring into the void that summer, I prayed and wished God would send me goodness and mercy.

Throughout my years of loneliness in the country, I learned to be really good at faking happiness. I was an actress, after all. I'd spent my youth bottling up my real emotions so no one accused me of being whiny or ungrateful. "But you have it so easy," my four siblings would say, repeating the same stories of our family's poor years before I was

13

born, back when they had to keep their feet on the seats of my dad's car because the floorboard was completely missing and they could see the asphalt rushing underneath them.

I'd kept up my act of happiness that terrible summer. I applied a smile with my red lipstick and brushed black mascara to make my dull eyes seem bright before heading to work at a credit union called WESLA, which served the employees at the Western Electric plant. On Fridays, I stuffed my toes into my tallest heels so I could priss down the plant's assembly line with a briefcase full of cash. "Shake that money, honey," the men called. I set up the briefcase on a table so the guys could cash their paychecks before heading home. I gorged on their attention and flirted aggressively. "You could really treat a girl right with that money," I'd say with a wink. Then I'd hop back in my car and cry all the way home. Bobo was too old to bite Freddy's tail so he lounged on the back porch. All my friends were married, engaged, in college, or had careers. I had no parties or dinners to attend. My parents were in bed before nine. My only standing date was rocking in the night, staring into the dark.

Donna came to visit at the end of summer. "You need to get out of here," Donna whispered one night. She had woken up to feed Daniel, or as she referred to him while she held her gut, "Absolutely my last child." She told me about Oklahoma City while she nursed him, occasionally wincing from the large baby's hungry mouth. Her church was full of single men. Successful, single men. And there were lots of jobs available. "It's like a real city," she finished.

Donna had made quite the romantic life for herself in Oklahoma City. She married a guy named Tim McCoy, the exact name of my dad's favorite old western movie star (no relation, sadly). Tim often reminded everyone that he was a self-proclaimed history buff and described Oklahoma City as the last great frontier city. He said it was an entire city settled in a single day by people desperate for a second chance.

So, I made my wish. I would leave my depression behind and travel to the bright and shining city on a hill. There, five hundred miles to the west, a man would rescue me from my broken heart. A company would recognize my talent and give me the job of my dreams. I'd find a deeper love, a fulfilling career, and a better life. All my dreams would come true in the magical land called Oklahoma City.

And I lied to myself by calling it hope.

MY INTERVIEW FELL into a relaxed conversation and it seemed like Kathy was about to give me the job. She joked about Oklahoma's weather. "We're so used to leaning into the wind, we'd all fall on our faces if it stopped." I laughed and smiled. She added, "You'll learn when you start walking around here."

"You know," I said during a lull in our conversation, "I had no idea federal employees were in a union."

"I'm sorry?" Kathy asked.

"Since this is a federal credit union," I said quickly, "I just didn't know federal agencies were in a labor union."

She shook her head. "No, that's not how this works," she said. "Credit unions have nothing to do with labor unions. Credit unions are a different type of financial institution that's owned by its members. We share our profits with the member-owners in the form of better rates on everything from checking accounts to loans. Credit unions were formed to serve a distinct community of closely-knit members. But, really, we've grown beyond the originating members to serve almost anyone connected to our community."

"Oh," I said, as if I understood. "I see, that's really interesting."

"There are credit unions for teachers, state employees, and there's a really big one called Tinker Federal Credit Union that services the military and workers at Tinker Air Force Base. Here," she gestured to the conference room, "we serve the federal employees and their families working in this building."

She gave me a brief history lesson of the Alfred P. Murrah Federal Building. It was built in 1977 and the Federal Employees Credit Union had been the very first tenant in the building. It was so small it couldn't afford a vault, so the DEA agents would stash the cash in their evidence room next to a few pounds of cocaine and confiscated assault rifles. Slowly, FECU (the acronym for Federal Employees Credit Union) built up its assets from nothing to over ten million dollars.

"Wow," I said, fidgeting in my seat. "I guess I never really understood it." I was anxious to leave the interview before I said something else stupid and Kathy changed her mind about giving me the job.

"It's fine," she said. "You wouldn't understand it unless you worked at-" her voice trailed off as she glanced at my resume. "How long did you work at WESLA?"

My throat gulped so loud it echoed. "Two years."

"Mmhmm," Kathy hummed, staring at my resume. "And did you ever attend college?"

My heart sank. I hadn't put my one year of college on my resume because no financial institution would hire me with a 0.5 GPA. Especially if they discovered I'd failed remedial math. Twice. I opened my mouth to make up some half-truth, but nothing came to mind. I was cornered and my thoughts started to spin. "It's a funny story," I started. "Kind of. Well, not really. You see-"

"Is this the new teller?" a woman asked from the doorway. She had a bright red perm and was smiling with an aura of vibrant and eager energy.

"It's our *first* interview," Kathy answered. I could tell this powerful woman was Kathy's boss, probably the CEO. And from Kathy's answer, I knew I'd blown it. There wouldn't be a second interview.

The CEO looked at me. "When were you born?"

"1967," I stammered.

"No, silly," she said, "What day? What month?"

"March thirty-first," I said slowly, then rushing at the end, "Ma'am."

The CEO looked at Kathy, "We need another Aries. Hire her."

So, I was hired. My first day on the job happened to be Halloween and Kathy told me I could wear a costume, but of course I knew better. I wasn't going to be the goofy girl dressed as a clown on my first day in a professional office. I arrived wearing a blue blazer over a cream blouse and below-knee skirt I'd bought over the weekend. I was met at the elevator by a tall witch with green skin and three ugly warts, one with hair sticking out of it.

"Let me show you around," the witch said. It was Kathy. Beautiful, blonde Kathy had transformed into an ugly witch with a hunched back. She hobbled around to introduce me. Housed on the third floor of a building designed for offices, FECU wasn't laid out like a traditional bank. There were no grand lobbies with lounging couches or oiled oak teller stalls with bronze bars. Instead, getting off the elevator, you'd never guess there was a credit union there. The walls had the same dull, cheap color from whatever contractor had submitted the lowest bid. The ceiling tiles were gray rectangles with black-pitted marks and plastic-covered fluorescent rods. Inside the metal-framed office doors were the operating units of the credit union. Inside one room was a teller line of burnt orange Formica. Another room had cubicles for loan officers and credit clerks. Florence Rogers, the CEO, had her private reception and office through another door.

I was introduced to a Ghostbuster, a mermaid, Snow White, Indiana Jones, and even a clown. They took me, the only girl wearing office clothes, down every hall of the nine-story building to pass out candy to the federal departments in the building. My toes ached while we chatted for a few minutes in the offices. Gruff agents with sun-hardened skin laughed at the costumes and showed us the newest pictures of their children. The trips up and down the halls felt more like a family reunion than a marketing pitch of fun-sized Hersheys and Twizzlers. Our last stop was the daycare on the second floor, where we emptied our buckets for cute little Caspers and Teenage Mutant Ninja Turtles.

"Halloween is a big deal here," the Ghostbuster told me, as if I hadn't noticed yet. On my second day at work, Kathy had to re-introduce me to everyone again because I couldn't recognize a single face.

I'D LIKE TO TELL you I appreciated my luck in the way Florence Rogers hired me. I'd like to describe how I returned Florence's favor by working hard for my new team. Or that I studied credit union operations and their history to avoid embarrassing myself like I had with Kathy. But that's not what happened. Instead, by my second month there, I had ticked off every coworker and typed up my two-weeks' notice.

It started with my shameless flirting. It was natural for me to fall into the role of the cute new girl. The sum of my professional career had been my catwalk down the factory floor at WESLA, so I immediately assumed the same personality and basked in the attention. These men were federal agents. Sure, some were social security officers with sizeable bellies and balding hair, but others worked for the ATF and the DEA. They spent the weeks and nights working out, firing guns, and going undercover in biker gangs and cartel rings. Their eyes were hard, like Kurt Russell, and their chests were thick. A few of the single guys and one married man asked me out. I played my part in the cycle of flirting, "Oh, I'm a little harder to catch than that." They loved it. I loved it. My colleagues . . . not so much.

Then I tattled on Stacy, the Ghostbuster girl who had showed me the ropes my first days at FECU. She'd asked me to do something that didn't follow the company procedures I'd just learned. Looking back now, it wasn't a big deal. Rather than correct her to the proper procedure, I did what she asked and immediately walked into Kathy's office to mention the wrong procedure was being taught. In a couple of hours, Kathy called us together to explain the proper procedure and that anyone caught doing differently would be reprimanded. I pretended to be shocked by Kathy's little talk but, of course, everyone knew what I'd done and they all liked Stacy better than me. The next day at work, one of the loan officers brushed by my teller stall and muttered, "Bitch."

I decided all the girls were mean and FECU was a toxic work environment. No one invited me to lunch. No one asked how my weekend was. My newness wore away and the guys stopped flirting with me. I sent my resume out to some other credit unions, ready to leave FECU behind.

After one lunch spent at a pay phone bank doing a phone interview with another credit union, Kathy asked me to train a new hire named Sonja. Sonja was around my age with a broad smile and all the trendy late '80s fashion: a perm with bangs and a beaded necklace that clicked whenever her head moved. She knew a couple of the employees at FECU and came over because her community bank was struggling. As she explained to me, small banks and credit unions across the country, and especially in Oklahoma, were closing. They were still suffering from the Penn Square Bank collapse and the more recent bankruptcy of First National Bank, which had owned and operated the second-tallest building downtown. It was an extremely hard time to be in finance in Oklahoma City and FECU was one of the exceptions to the general demise of financial institutions. Within a few minutes of meeting, Sonja asked, "Why would you move to Oklahoma City?"

I'd heard the same question from others since my interview with Kathy. Turns out, it wasn't an accusation at all. Most people were genuinely shocked by a young woman choosing to move into Oklahoma City at a time everyone else was moving away. The oil and gas bust in the early '80s left the city decimated with no jobs or companies with profitable futures. It seemed like Oklahoma City, one of the youngest cities in America, would soon revert to a true frontier city with tent neighborhoods and horse-drawn carriages. Years later, when I met our mayor and told him my story of moving, he joked and said, "So you're the one." Apparently, in my desperate pursuit of a new life, I'd been the one person who jumped onto the Titanic when everyone else was elbowing for a seat on the lifeboats.

Sonja's quick wit and no-nonsense attitude quickly earned her the respect and friendship of most of the girls in the office. Since I worked next to her on the teller line, we became close, which forced the other girls to accept me. It was my first time being in a clique of women. The dark years in Shreveport started to dissolve in my mind as I discovered a rich kaleidoscope of friendships. It was like a quilt wrapped around me, warming the cold edges of my soul and healing the lonely wounds of my heart. I stayed at FECU, feeling like I'd finally found my home.

Looking back, I guess it was natural for me to find my community at FECU. It was the community center of the whole building. As a credit union serving federal employees, it didn't have massive business credit lines. It had car and home loans for federal employees, backed by small, twenty-dollar savings account deposits. We got to know the lives behind the faces of almost every employee in the building through their transactions. We knew how big their home was, where it was, and whether they built or bought. We knew the cars they drove. We knew who put aside money for their children's college funds and when they married.

We all have a natural fear of intimacy and nothing is more intimate than your personal finances. The forced intimacy thrust into the hands of a stiff-collared businessman in a bank is awkward, uncomfortable, and unnatural. It's hard to trust their promise of giving you the best available interest rate when you know Wall Street is making a profit on your loan. When you close the transaction, it is sometimes hard to tell if the smile on the officer's face is because you've accomplished a dream, or because he's just met his quota for the quarter.

But at credit unions like FECU, every major transaction feels like a shared celebration. Every house loan closed is a victory for every other member of the credit union. Every account has an equal vote on choosing who serves on the board of directors. That volunteer board works for free and decides how the credit union spends the excess revenue. Credit unions transform the awkward financial intimacy into a shared community. In a federal government stacked with immovable bureaucracies, FECU was the one place the members had a voice. FECU held their trust first and their money second. It connected employees from every agency in the building into the same pool of shared success. If a community could ever be considered a body, FECU was the warm, pumping heart of the Alfred P. Murrah Federal Building.

Still, it was embarrassing for me to admit FECU was the warm heart of my life. If I was asked, I called Sonja my best friend in those years. If you had asked Sonja, she wouldn't have called me her *best* friend. Except for a few times we had baby showers at someone's house, our only time spent together was at work. Sonja was married with a daughter and was very close with her sister. She had a full, vibrant life of fun and love outside work. If I left FECU for another job, the joy in her life would have continued. For me, however, leaving FECU would have snuffed out the only joy in my life.

I knew something was wrong with that. It wasn't normal for me to consider Monday mornings as the highlight of my week. Particularly when I had a husband at home.

2017 Ironman Arizona

Minute One

SWIMMING MAY BE the shortest leg of an Ironman, but it's the most difficult to learn. Running is a natural, instinctive human movement. Anyone who has seen a snake slither across the lawn knows running can happen in an instant and without any intentional thought. The cycling motion is easy, too, once you get your balance. You lock your shoes into the pedals and the mechanics force your legs to move in only one way. But there is nothing natural about dunking your head into water and there are no contraptions to guide your flailing arms and legs.

Swimming is almost all technique over effort. You have to stay mindful of every angle and muscle in your body. You start by stretching flat on the water with your face submerged. When you take a stroke, you're supposed to leave your elbow bent like a hinge as you push your arm downwards, kind of like climbing a horizontal ladder. When you reach for your next stroke, you're supposed to keep your hand close to your side with your thumb grazing your ribs. So, it's like climbing a horizontal ladder in a narrow tunnel. Your knees should be stiff with your feet making small kicks, so it's like climbing a horizontal ladder in a narrow tunnel with your legs stuck in a bucket. For every stroke you are supposed to kick your feet six times on the water, which means you have to maintain a more difficult rhythm than tapping your head and rubbing your belly.

Oh, and I almost forgot, you're supposed to breathe occasionally. Every two or three strokes you change all of your technique and roll your body to one side, dropping your shoulder to open your chest, and take a quick breath. If you have the proper form, the top of your head should create a kind of wake in the water in front of your mouth so, with perfect form, you end up lowering your jaw to breathe the little air bubble created by your head. But make sure you keep kicking your legs in that barrel, though, because if you slow down the air bubble will collapse and you'll inhale water.

Even with all that, I had full confidence when I dunked my head into Lake Tempe. I had spent more time training with a coach on my swimming than cycling or running. For months, I had been swimming laps around the shore of an Oklahoma City lake with my husband paddling next to me in a kayak. I was comfortable with my form and could keep all the nuanced angles of my body in line. In my first strokes in Lake Tempe, I felt prepared to propel myself the full 2.4 miles.

But in my third stroke, someone's arm slammed the back of my head.

My goggles shifted and water stung my eyes. I choked and sputtered a curse as I coughed. I gasped as I shifted my goggles to dump out the water and the waves slapped my open mouth, making me choke on more water. I kicked my legs hard to stay above the waves and set my goggles and swim cap back in place. I still couldn't get a deep breath, so I rolled over to start a slow side-stroke and inhale the clear air.

One minute into my impossible race and I was already bruised, out of breath, and lagging behind my friends.

CHAPTER TWO

Sinking

IT WAS A SETUP from the beginning. Donna and Tim had arranged it. A week or so before I moved to Oklahoma City, they'd convinced me to visit. There was a guy at church they wanted me to meet. The guy picked me up Saturday night and away we went. His car was immaculate and smelled brand new. He was nice and respectful. And funny. I laughed so much my cheeks hurt. I needed funny to lift me out of my brooding in Shreveport. He'd just graduated from Bible college and was going to be a pastor.

Bingo.

"Well?" Donna asked me the next morning. We were in her kitchen. Somehow I'd slept in, even though Daniel had cried to be fed and changed at four in the morning.

"Well, what?" I tried to say casually, spilling some coffee from the pot as I giggled. "First, it got kind of awkward," I started. "After we ate at Olive Garden, we went to the state fair and got on the monorail—"

"WHOOSH!" One of Donna's kids, an orange-haired toddler, waved his arm in a big circle.

Donna shooed him away. "Sorry, he's the dramatic one," she said.

I thought all her sons were equally loud and obnoxious, but whatever.

"Well," I continued, "it was so packed we were squished together on the bench. So—"

"WHOOSH!" the carrot-top boy screamed again, waving his arm in an even bigger circle.

A voice from a terrifying depth in Donna's chest erupted, "I told you to play in your room!" The kid ran away, crying.

"Anyway," I said, "so, like, we haven't even held hands and here we are, our thighs smashed, pressed together in a side hug—"

"WHOOSH!"

This time Donna got up and chased the hellion into his bedroom. I sipped my coffee and promised myself for the hundredth time to never have kids. Donna called from the hallway for help. I walked over and my bare feet felt the carpet turn cold and soggy. The toilet had clogged and was gushing water out of the bathroom and into the hall. We frantically tried to stop it, our pajamas soaked in toilet water as we lifted the porcelain top and jiggled every lever we could find.

That was the first of many warnings I ignored. I had been so focused on describing a date that I'd ignored someone literally screaming in my face that something was wrong. More warnings would come and, just like that morning, I intentionally ignored them all. I was so fixated on securing a husband that I was willfully blind to any possible danger.

Often in youth groups, us girls had been separated from the boys. I don't know what the boys were told, but we were reminded to be good and pretty so we could serve our God-fearing husbands. Before you judge my church, that attitude wasn't solely a Christianity thing. It was just the Christian version of the original Disney fairy tales. Women were born into captivity, and only a prince with a sword could slay our dragon and set us free. The Christian man just carried a Bible, which, funny enough, was often called the Sword of the Lord. In my depression of losing Seth, failing college, and rocking alone as I stared into the void, I was convinced that I needed a Christian prince to slay my demons for me.

The soon-to-be pastor full of jokes in Oklahoma City checked all the boxes of a Christian prince. He proposed within my first three months in Oklahoma City. It was Christmas Eve and my whole family was together. My sister Camille announced her engagement the same night. Of course, she'd had a proper courtship over the past year. But I didn't care to wait. I'd done enough sitting and waiting in Shreveport for three proper courtships. Besides, Donna and Tim got engaged in their first six weeks together and they were living a modern frontier romance. So, I said yes without any hesitation and we scheduled the ceremony in March. We'd be married within six months of our first date.

We chose to get married in Oklahoma City at Donna's church, where my fiancé had attended his whole life. His pastor couldn't officiate because of a vacation he'd planned. We all loved him and were disappointed until one week before the wedding. He called Donna one evening and warned she needed to do anything possible to discourage me from the wedding, for my own sake. After a hurricane of angry calls between my fiancé, his family, my mom, Donna, and everyone else, I had only four words repeating in my mind: *to heck with him*. Nobody would stop me from walking down the aisle. Nobody would make me move back into my sister's house to sleep on the floor next to an infant. Nobody would drag me back to Shreveport to stare at the longleaf pines in the night. My better life was finally within sight. I'd found a Christian prince who could make me laugh. Soon, I'd get to quit my job at FECU and be a pastor's wife. I didn't need a college degree to bake a casserole or host a prayer breakfast. This marriage was my only chance for a rescue.

"But it doesn't seem like you love him," my friend Mary told me the night before the ceremony.

I paused for a moment. Her words were no revelation. I'd had the same thought since my first date six months earlier. "He's a really good guy. We'll learn to love each other." I paused and repeated a line I'd heard from a romantic movie. Or maybe it was from a Disney fairy tale. "We have the rest of our lives to figure that part out."

The sanctuary had some repairs being done, which now seemed like a dubious reason given the pastor's opinion of our marriage, so we had the ceremony in a classroom with a low ceiling and fluorescent lights. I walked down a flowerless aisle of plastic chairs in a borrowed wedding dress. My two brothers, Mike and Alan, weren't there. They were both busy men and could only take time off for one wedding. They'd both chosen to attend Camille's wedding six weeks later because, to be fair, Camille had given them the proper notice to plan for their trip.

The officiant was a youth pastor who looked more nervous than me. No one cheered when we kissed. A few people laughed. Our reception was in the youth group's kitchen with painted brick walls. We flew to San Antonio for our honeymoon. I had waited for that night my whole life, but after midnight I stared at the ceiling while my husband slept. I felt ashamed because, as it turned out, I felt the same inside. Empty and alone.

"It was a mistake," I told my mom a few months later. We sat in my car in her circle driveway, the evening light resting on her wild roses and tall sunflowers.

"Of course you think that," my mom said. "We all do, at first. It will pass." On the eight-hour drive back to Oklahoma City, I stopped three times for a hamburger, pizza, Kentucky Fried Chicken, and two giant Diet Cokes.

My husband never became a pastor and my feeling never passed. He had a brief stint as a volunteer youth pastor at a small church with maybe ten kids. It didn't pay anything and we had to mop the rented space after Wednesday night and Sunday morning services. There were no casseroles or prayer breakfasts. Before long, we left. We obviously couldn't go back to Donna's church since the pastor didn't approve of our marriage. After a time, we gave up and stayed home on Sunday mornings to watch movies and eat donuts.

And I gained 100 pounds in our first year together.

THE EMPTINESS I felt at home matched the emptiness I found in the churches we visited. There were lots of smiles and quick jokes, but no deep connections, no authentic despair, and no genuine love. I discovered the Christian story, like the Disney fairy tale, had been a myth all along. If the Bible was a sword, it was a polished sword hanging above a mantel. It was something pretty to look at, but it had never been brandished in a real, raw fight. I felt fooled by the false hopes preached on Sunday mornings. My mom's lullaby promising goodness and mercy was a lie, just like her promise that my feeling would pass. I felt no goodness, no mercy, and no joy.

So, if I gained a few pounds, it didn't really matter. The least I deserved in the aftermath of a lifetime of lies was the comfort of butter-crusted bread and a sweet drink. Even if I'd pulled a bait-and-switch on my husband, growing from the cute thin girl into a size larger than he'd ever fathomed, he had failed me first. He was supposed to save me but, years into our marriage, my demons still sneered and swirled around me.

Besides, the weight gain wasn't my fault. It started with my mom. She lorded over the pantry like an obsessed accountant. Being the last child in the house, it was easy for her to know exactly what I ate. She'd check the cabinets in the evening and shoot me a knowing look. She never said the words, but I felt her eyes telling me, *No one will love you if you eat that much.* She'd frown when my dad and I packed cookies and sodas for our Saturday trots on the horses into the country. Her accusations turned sugar into a kind of forbidden fruit, and I craved it. When I was finally free in Oklahoma City, devouring the juicy burgers and creamy shakes was pure ecstasy in the absence of my mom's ever-judging stare.

Then there was my genetics. My sister Camille had gained an aggressive amount of weight after she'd graduated from college. We had an aunt who died from a weight issue. Something ran in the family that affected our thyroids. Camille and I were designed at birth to be big-boned girls. There was nothing wrong with it and there was nothing I could do about it. No matter the exercise plan or Weight Watchers meals, the weight stayed. I saw no reason to fight a battle I was doomed to lose. The smarter play was to avoid the war altogether and enjoy some peace with a Vanilla Coke.

Besides, I needed the energy to focus at work. I was a career girl now that my husband wasn't going to be a pastor. I needed my focus to survive the day, even if a blind man could have done my job better than me.

As it turned out, failing remedial math (twice) wasn't a fluke. I had trouble balancing my drawer every day, which was basically my only job. Even though tellers had other duties to perform around the credit union, I always found a way out of them. For example, there was a printer by the teller desks for printing account statements. It was a huge early printer that made a kind of scratching sound when the thick serrated paper with green and white stripes fed through the plastic panels. Occasionally, the paper would go out and it was our job, as tellers, to replace it.

Except I never did. I'd know it was getting low and I'd convince the member at my desk a statement wasn't needed. Or I'd shuffle to the restroom when another teller was trying to print. If someone caught me and I had no escape, I'd meander over and start lifting the panels and touching the machine in random spots.

"Amy," the receptionist called once, "you're just switching the power button on and off."

"What's that again?" I'd ask with my sweetest voice. "You know, for whatever reason, my dumb brain can't figure it out."

The receptionist came and started to replace the paper. As I walked away with a satisfied smile, I heard her whisper, "Yeah, you're dumb like a fox."

She had figured me out. I spent all my energy manipulating others so I could avoid work. Pity is powerful and I abused it often. A big girl with a sweet voice could get a lot of help. I convinced myself I deserved it because I had a weight problem I couldn't control and no life outside of work.

There was a snack bar on the fourth floor, right above us, where we would often eat lunch. It was run by a blind man named Raymond. I don't know how a blind man could run a cash drawer for the snack bar, but apparently he always made his cash balance. No one in the federal building ever cheated him. One day, Raymond clicked his cane into our teller line and approached me. "Amy," he started before I could speak, having memorized my place on the line, "how are you today?" We had some small talk before getting to business. As he often did, he handed me a twenty-dollar bill. "Just need some ones, please." I fumbled in my drawer for a roll of 20 one-dollar-bills, barely able to see over my ballooned chest. "You're a saint," Raymond said as I handed him the roll.

Fifteen minutes later, Raymond clicked his cane against the door frame again. "What's going on Raymond?" I asked with a loud voice. It had been a boring afternoon and I was glad for an interesting story to tell the girls later. It's the small things that make work interesting, and the day Raymond came to my stall twice in an hour was a small nugget worth a moment of gossip.

Raymond leaned over the teller desk and whispered, "I think you gave me the wrong roll." He reached out and opened his hand, revealing a roll of $100 bills. I had handed Raymond two thousand dollars in exchange for his twenty bucks. My face burned as I dumped the large bills back into my drawer and handed Raymond the correct roll of ones. "Perfect," Raymond said a little louder, intentionally letting others hear him to try to mask my mistake, "Glad there is enough in my checking to cover it."

I wasn't joking before. Literally, a blind man was better at my job. Sonja and Stacy, the girl I had tattled on, were next to me on the teller line. I knew they'd heard, but they didn't tell anyone. I would have been fired in an instant if Kathy had found out. Even if we'd gotten the money back, handing two thousand dollars to a blind man would certainly be the last mistake a teller made while still employed in a credit union as small as ours.

And yet, as crazy as it sounds, I still cried when I was passed over for promotions. Every time, I blamed the management for having a conspiracy against me, preferring the prettier, thinner girls based only on looks. I would sob at home in anger and shame, convincing myself of everything except the truth.

WORKING AT FECU felt like living in some kind of movie, especially when we walked downtown for lunch. Oklahoma City's skyscrapers dwarfed the small offices in little ol' Shreveport. I gaped up and wondered how someone could work thirty stories high in an Oklahoma wind so strong it could tear the door off a car. There were glass skywalks and an underground tunnel system with restaurants and small shops that connected the downtown towers. Everything felt new and modern. Passing the lawyers in suits with our group of girls made me feel like Meg Ryan in *Sleepless in Seattle*. For a country girl like me, I was living a metropolitan dream.

I remember in 1991, the whole city seemed to share the same high esteem. We were a finalist in a very public competition to secure eighteen thousand new jobs. United Airlines needed to build a new, major repair center and opened bidding for cities to compete. Near the end of the deadline, there was no comparing the offer Oklahoma City waved in the air. In the center of the conservative state of Oklahoma, our city voted with overwhelming approval to tax ourselves. Over one hundred sixty *million* dollars would be generated in the new tax, held exclusively for the benefit of United Airlines. They just had to submit an invoice and the money was theirs.

It sounded like a bribe, and maybe it was. It also sounded desperate, and maybe that was true, too. The oil and gas bust in the eighties had destroyed the city's economy and we'd been trying for a decade to infuse our city with jobs that weren't tied to the price of oil. In 1989, we'd hosted the Olympic Festival, which coincided with the hundredth anniversary of the founding of Oklahoma City. In that relatively short span, we'd grown from a smattering of propped tents to hosting a nationally televised festival showcasing America's greatest athletes.

The repair center was the ticket we needed to hurdle away from our past and into a brighter, more secure future. Over seventy percent of the city agreed to pitch in. Think about that for a second. Over seventy percent of a city agreed to pay money out of their own pocket so some stranger could secure a job at the repair center. We all knew Oklahoma City had a problem and we wanted United Airlines to save us.

On the day of United Airlines' announcement, the CEO called our mayor and told the truth. No other proposal had come close to ours. We had knocked their socks off. But, unfortunately, they were declining our offer and choosing Indianapolis instead.

No one could understand how United could refuse us. We whispered accusations. Someone paid the CEO off. The labor union mafia intimidated the company to keep the jobs in the North. A few members on the board were caught in a dirty club and were blackmailed. As the weeks wore on, the painful truth came out and it was worse than any rumor. Apparently, United Airlines had discreetly sent some of their employees to Oklahoma City for a weekend to scout the city's culture. These secret visitors were given a company credit card to revel in whatever they could find. After a full weekend, they reported back on Monday with an empty expense report.

There had been nothing fun to enjoy.

Oklahoma City, they reported, was a wasteland of cold concrete and empty buildings. No music. No theaters. No curbside restaurants. No local pubs with unique brews. No coffee shops with a lake view. No bike lanes. No running trails. They had searched all around, practically waving cash above their heads down the empty streets, and found nothing to do and nobody to meet. It was a boring weekend. Depressing, even. And the United Airlines board refused to force their employees to live in the lifeless limbo of Oklahoma City.

Ouch. It was like a searing iron driven into the gut of the city. Our feet stopped racing. We stumbled off the track. The city let out a collective exhale, releasing all the spirit and momentum from the Olympic Festival. We'd been accused of having no soul. And even though we denied it out loud, we knew it was true in our own hearts. The Olympic Festival had been an act, a Wild West pony trick in a ghost town of storefronts carrying no inventory. We were a suburban city without a center—all extremities and no heart. And, apparently, we couldn't pay someone enough money to move here.

WE LIKE TO BLAME others for our false hopes. Oklahoma City blamed United Airlines for giving us the false hope of a repair center. They asked for offers and we gave them the best one. How could they say no? I blamed my husband for the false hope of marriage. I blamed him for not being a pastor. I blamed the management at work for not being promoted. I blamed my mom and my genetics for my weight gain. Mostly, I blamed God for how quickly my life had dropped from bad to worse in Oklahoma City. Then I stopped blaming God altogether because, as I'd discovered, goodness and mercy was also false.

We experience false hope when we fundamentally misunderstand what hope means. False hope exists when we have a dream or fantasy and, without any work on our part, we give it the name of hope. False hope is the woman who uses student loans to buy lottery tickets, whispering, "I hope I win." There is no mistaking that woman is betting her life on a fantasy.

False hope is when you're scrolling through Instagram and see that perfect picture of a bikini body on a beach with a husband stacked with muscles and children smiling with all their teeth. You see the picture and think, *I hope we'll be like that one day.* Then you eat a cheeseburger with a large ice cream shake. False hope is the business conference you immediately shell out a few hundred bucks to attend because, somewhere in your mind, you are hoping you'll meet someone at the conference who will change your life forever.

In those early days in Oklahoma City, I hadn't learned my lesson in hope yet. The truth is hope has nothing to do with somebody doing something for you or some event happening to you. It has everything to do with you and only you. No one else. If you are hoping your husband will rescue you from yourself, you're believing a lie. If you are hoping to get a promotion when you won't bother learning to change the printer paper, you're dreaming. When Oklahoma City passed a tax hoping United Airlines would magically fix its failing economy, it was a fantasy.

Having a wish and calling it *hope* can inflict a lot of damage in your life. We become confused when our wishes don't come true and we start believing hope is as weak as our fantasies. When people coach us to have hope, we ignore the call because we think they are telling us to have dreams, which never come true. When we belittle hope, we cripple ourselves.

If you happen to be stubborn and continue dreaming, reality has a way of repeatedly waking you up. Every time we are hit with the harsh truth of reality, it leaves us dazed and, often, angry. The repeated blows start to numb our souls, and our simmering anger creates a bitter, critical view of the world. Over time, we stop believing in the dreams we falsely called *hope* and we start telling ourselves different stories. We see the happy family on the beach and say, "That's fake and I bet her husband is sleeping with the nanny." We see a new business opening with a staged picture of patrons and think, *It won't last.* We ignore the business conference because we know, deep inside, nothing will change. We start to believe this life is simply random interactions between the lucky and the unlucky. We start to believe we are all ships without rudders, our sails twisted by whatever winds blow, and our hulls tossed by whatever currents flow, defenseless against whatever storm may strike.

IN 1993, two years before the Oklahoma City bombing, we moved into an adobe-style rent house. Like other houses on our street, the windows were protected by black metal bars. I did some gardening in the backyard and, even in April, the humid air was so hot I felt like an egg being poached. Well, actually, I sat on the bench with the strong legs while my skinny nephews pulled weeds. And, well, maybe it was more like pulling straight grass because I hadn't planted anything yet. But I was supervising and paying them five bucks an hour so, really, I was doing them a favor.

I took a break from the heat for a Sonic run, changing out of my sweat-soaked extra-extra-extra-large t-shirt before squeezing into our car and blasting the air and radio playing Reba and Vince's *The Heart Won't Lie*. I couldn't tell you what kind of car we had, but whatever it was, it was new. Having new cars meant we usually couldn't afford two cars, but we made it work and the FECU girls often gave me a ride to work.

At Sonic, a cute blonde teenager in mid-thigh shorts brought my drinks and mid-afternoon snack: a steak finger dinner with fries and a thick, crispy piece of warm Texas toast. Her hair was slicked from sweat and somehow her makeup still looked flawless. Or maybe she didn't need makeup. I asked for all my change back, no tip.

The boys pulled the grass all day, which was ridiculous. I had wanted to plant some Mexican petunias or yellow yarrow before Donna picked them up. They'd have to come back over again tomorrow and, of course, Donna wouldn't drop them off until after church. I thought about spending tomorrow morning positioning the flats of flowers exactly where they needed to be. They'd only have to dig a quick hole and plant the things. I hated doing that. Sunday was supposed to be my one day off to relax.

I was glad I didn't have children. If they still couldn't do an honest day's work at this age, what was the point? I'd hosted a baby shower for Sonja a few months ago. She'd gotten pregnant six months after giving birth to her first daughter. Before we opened her presents, she pulled me aside and said, "Why is God doing this to me?" Anxiety tortured her forehead and I fumbled something to the tune of *children are a blessing* before walking away. I thought it was a terrible thing for a mother to say about her yet-to-be-born daughter and I was reminded, yet again, that nothing good came from having children.

"Thank you very much," I said as I snatched the remote from my husband. It was the least he could give me after all the yard work I was doing. I switched the channels because we'd already watched *Die Hard* a hundred times by now, but all the major channels were still running clips and stories from a standoff down in Waco, Texas. A bunch of religious zealots had died trying to fight off the FBI or something. Some women and children had died.

"That's just crazy," I said. *But then again*, I thought, *I know something about religious lies. Sometimes you believe them and your life is destroyed.* I flipped back to the movie. At least Bruce Willis had his shirt off.

A few days later at work, a member came in with his arm in a sling. "Did the bad guys get you?" I tried to joke. These tough men had a different kind of humor I'd grown accustomed to. I guess they had to be a little rough in their jokes to survive the intensity of their lines of duty.

The member gave a brief smile with sad eyes and lifted his slung arm with a wince, "I was in Waco. They got a lot of us."

My face burned hot with embarrassment and I started to apologize. I hadn't considered some Oklahoma agents had been called to help in Waco. The member was polite and told me it was alright. He tapped the stack of bills I'd given him and paused, as if he was about to say something else, then walked away. He didn't have the heart to explain the details I pieced together over the next few days. He didn't know how to explain what it was like to watch his friends die on a gravel road or to hear the screaming women and children burned inside that terrible compound.

2017 Ironman Arizona

Hour Two

IN A POOL, swimming straight is easy because the water is clear and there's a blue line at the bottom to orient yourself. But in the murky water of a natural lake like Lake Tempe, it was a little more difficult to stay on course. I had to lift my head high above the waves to spot the big yellow buoys marking the path. Often, the current or my own bad form took me off course. Besides being annoyed that I was in the wrong spot, having to course correct meant I'd just added more distance to my overall swim. After a few screw-ups in the water, my 2.4-mile swim was another hundred meters farther. Then after a few more mistakes, two hundred meters farther. Maybe that wouldn't be such a big deal if I wasn't racing against the clock.

You see, every leg of the triathlon was precisely timed with a small chip attached to my ankle. At periodic stations on the course, my time was updated in real time on the official Ironman website and mobile app for anyone to track my progress, including race officials. If I failed to cross one of the stations before the set cut-off time, I'd be disqualified from the race. They'd take my chip away and update the website and app. My time stamp would disappear and, instead, be replaced with those three dreaded letters: DNF. Did. Not. Finish.

Failing to finish is not a disappointment. It's not embarrassing. It's devasting. Many of us had trained for over a year. More than fifty-two weeks of sore legs and arms. Over 365 days of walking funny in recovery. Almost a thousand hours of swimming, biking, and running. For over a full year, I'd sacrificed half of every Saturday and Sunday to training. For over a year, I hadn't had that second glass of wine on Friday night. I'd left dinners without dessert to be in bed by eight. When Donna or my friends frowned at my early exit, I proclaimed it was all worth it. I was going to complete an Ironman.

And if I missed just one cut-off time, all of it was for nothing. DNF on the official tracker would be like a violet tattoo on my forehead. Sure, everyone would say it was okay. "At least you tried," they'd console. "It was impressive that you tried in the first place." But to me, I felt like a DNF would render my entire year meaningless. It meant the best effort of my life came up short. It meant I was a fake athlete. It meant for all my talk, I was still weak and fragile.

Fear is a powerful emotion but it can only take you so far. I'd obsessed about a DNF for a year and yet, an hour and a half into the swim, I wasn't thinking about it anymore. I was tired and breathless, my arms were burning, and I still had over a mile more to swim. The cut-off time for the swim was two hours and twenty minutes, which meant I had less than an hour to swim the final mile.

I stopped to tread water and orient myself. The water was white with the splashes of athletes leading to the shore where a crowd cheered. I knew my husband was in that crowd. So was my coach. So were my friends. I knew by the time I got out, my Okie training buddies would be there, too.

I dunked my head back into the lake and renewed my stroke. My only driving thought was to meet my friends to enjoy a dry towel, a sports drink, and something delicious like pickles or half frozen Uncrustables. Whenever I swallowed lake water and choked, I didn't shift into my side stroke. Instead, I pushed on in full strokes, imagining my friend Chris was calling my name from the shore. When my arms turned to noodles with no energy, I thought of Ruth's beaming smile next to me on the bike. She had a form of leukemia that lasted forever but she still showed up today. She had convinced me to sign up for this thing to begin with. If she could do a triathlon with leukemia, I could do one with tired arms. My body ached but I pulled and kicked harder. I wouldn't let my friends down. I would give them everything I had.

And, one hour of floundering later, I made it.

I limped up the ramp with some help from volunteers in purple shirts steadying my arms and hands. To me, the monotone beep from the time mat sounded like cathedral bells ringing victory. Another group of volunteers laid me down to unzip and peel off my wetsuit. It took maybe three seconds for them to quickly take it off. I felt like a grown baby on a changing table with my legs in the air, but in case you couldn't tell by now, triathletes have a high tolerance for impolite and slightly vulgar situations.

I jogged barefoot into the cycling transition. The metal racks were almost empty so it was easier than ever to spot my pink-framed bike. I peeled off my swim cap, took off my goggles, pulled out my ear plugs, dried off with a towel, ate an Uncrustable, drank some water with salt, shifted socks over my damp feet, slid into my cycling shoes, dried off again with the towel because my sweat was dripping again, put on arm warmers, clipped my helmet onto my head, munched on a few pickles, took another long drink of water, stuffed my hands into my cycling gloves, and adjusted the earpieces of my sunglasses under my helmet's straps. It only took me twelve minutes. Then I trotted with my bike past the next beeping gateway, hopped on my bike, and clipped my shoes into the pedals.

"I'm winning!" I yelled at a camera crew whizzing by on a moped. I laughed at my hilarious joke because I was clearly in the very back of the pack and, you know, I'm clearly the funniest person ever. I adjusted my sunglasses and focused on the desert road, trying to find one of my Okie friends.

I didn't know that while I laughed into the camera, my friend Chris was getting out of the water ten seconds after the cut-off. The volunteers didn't lay him down to take off his wetsuit. Instead, they unstrapped his ankle time chip and informed him of his DNF. Ruth was still in the water, unaware that each strained stroke was for nothing. My training buddies were out. Their Ironman race was over.

Chapter Three

Pit of Darkness, Well of Light

APRIL 19, 1995:

"I look like a big ole' sunflower!" Sonja waved her arms in a bright yellow dress suit. I wanted to assure her, to tell her she was wearing a woman power suit like a model on the cover of a magazine. But I laughed instead. She was so right. The blazer and skirt were as radiant as that sunny Wednesday morning, three days after Easter with fresh leaves shimmering on the elm in the parking lot across the street. I was wasting my first hour of the day walking around to show off pictures of the new house we'd built. We were closing the next morning and my giddiness couldn't be bottled in my office chair.

Closing on the house was like a dream for me. After all these years, my husband and I were going to own a brick house with three bedrooms, open kitchen plan, and an entire backyard begging for a good spring planting. Tomorrow, the painting of my life would be complete. I was only twenty-eight and I couldn't ask for anything more.

"Did you remember?" Claudette asked. She been asking for months for a few daffodil bulbs and knew I'd been in Shreveport over the weekend to snip some flowers from my mom's garden.

"Yeah, they're somewhere in a box or something," I said. Then I showed her pictures of the bathrooms and considered my couch options. A sectional was good but it closed off the space and, you know, a girl like me needs some space to move around. Someone mentioned a modern style of couch. A minimalist approach with four thin legs that could never handle my weight. "I think modern is ugly," I said.

"My windflowers are finally blooming," Kim Burgess mentioned after flipping a second time through my pictures.

"I told you the compost would work," I said. "Plant some tulips and you'll have a nice layered effect." We were huddled over Kim's desk, which adjoined Florence's office. I peeked and noticed all the department heads assembling in front of Florence's desk. It looked like they were about to have a meeting, which meant I should probably act like I worked here. I almost ran into Vicky in the hallway. I moved left and she moved the same direction. For a few seconds, we did a little mirror dance with a giggle before I gave a dramatic curtsy for her to pass. She gave an equally dramatic nod of royal gratitude.

As soon as I plopped into my chair, Robbin came in my office. She eased into Patti's chair next to me and rubbed her belly. I was annoyed and wished Patti had been here to deflect Robbin. She probably needed to ask about the credit card status of some member. I thought it was rude for her to barge in before I got settled, even though it was already nine o'clock. She could have just called me. I bet she was headed to the bathroom and decided to stop by here first. I swear she had to pee like three times an hour. I made another mental note that I never wanted to get pregnant.

She started to say something but my phone rang. I mouthed an apology and answered. It was my husband. He wanted us to buy a new truck. I thought about how much more debt it would create, especially since we were about to add a hefty mortgage, but then again, who cared? We were closing on our house tomorrow. Nothing could get me down. I transferred him to my friend Karan in the loan department.

Robbin leaned over as soon as my receiver was down. I fumbled in my drawer, trying to stall, but eventually looked up. She was beaming with her hands on her stomach. It was probably the natural glow of being in her third trimester, but I thought there was more. She looked anxious to share something wonderful with me.

But she never would.

It was like a thousand speakers blasted a hundred tones of deep bass. My eyes clamped. I wasn't sure if I spun, or if the world spun around me. The raging distortion whirled in my ribcage as I felt myself fall. Without thinking, I screamed the sinner's prayer as fast as I could, "Dear-Lord-Jesus-I-know-I-am-sinner-and-I-ask--"

In an instant, I wasn't falling.

I heard a woman shrieking someplace distant.

I heard a loud popping sound.

Then I discovered it was me. I was the woman screaming.

I couldn't see. It felt like shattered bits of my teeth were grinding against my gums. Something weighed on my waist. I banged my head against a solid wall. I jerked, but nothing happened. My arms didn't respond. I tried to shift my leg, my hand, my knee, my neck, but I couldn't budge. I was encased. Eyes open or shut, there was a void of absolute dark. A sweltering heat made it hard to breathe. Even when I caught a breath, there was a vile stench simmering in the burnt air, a mix of soured blood and defecation. I gagged, desperate for more air, and also desperate to never inhale that stench again.

My first thought was *I didn't say it fast enough. I'm in Hell.* My second thought was *Maybe I was shot in the back of the head.* I heard scurrying footsteps above me. The shrieks subsided and it got quiet, perfectly still, save for a single moan somewhere very close. My head pounded. I couldn't move my hands to wipe the foaming spittle from my chin.

A building alarm sounded far away. The quick, shrill sound brought me a moment of comfort. I wasn't in Hell. I was still alive.

For now.

I ran my tongue across my teeth, finding they seemed intact.

"Someone help!" I coughed out. Bits of concrete spewed from my mouth. "Robbin, I'm here. Robbin?" Maybe she could pull me out. Why wasn't she helping?

I considered something bigger had happened. *A tornado?* But the tornado sirens hadn't sounded. It had been pretty outside. *An earthquake? A nuclear explosion?* I was the last person alive. Everyone was dead. I would have to suffer here, alone, the last woman on Earth buried under the rubble of humanity.

I shook hard, trying to inch my body out of whatever was piled on me. In a few moments, my skin started to crawl with a tingling sensation. I couldn't feel my legs or arms anymore. All I felt was a slight pressure, like a sustained tension on my bones, wherever the concrete squeezed me. The heat was so intense I thought my skin should have glowed like a lump of coal in a campfire. The only way I could take a full breath was to lift my head upwards. I'd muster a few deep breaths of the disgusting air and scream for help again and again. No one replied. No one called back.

I started to whimper "Lord, though I walk in the valley of the shadow of death--" But I couldn't remember the rest of the verses. Surely, there was hope in that psalm. That's what the Bible was all about, right? But hope escaped me. I repeated versions of that first line. *I walk in the valley of the shadow. The valley of shadow and death.*

"This is where the daycare babies should be," a man's voice called.

"Here, I'm here!" I screamed.

"I hear you, child. How old are you?" The voice was calm and distant.

My fear and anxiety were interrupted for a moment. I was almost embarrassed. The man was at such ease, his tone so soft. *Had I been dreaming?*

"Um, I'm sorry," I said politely, "I'm twenty-eight."

"I think we have a live one," the man yelled. I called to him a few more times as he moved around to find me.

"I think I have your hand," he finally yelled. My numb hand felt a slight strain around my knuckles. Apparently, my right arm was stuck behind me in an awkward angle.

"You do," I called back.

"What color is your blouse?" the man asked.

I didn't know how to respond. His question was surreal. Like he wasn't human. *I'm buried, dude. My clothes are toast.*

"Ma'am, what color is your blouse?"

"Green?"

His voice leapt an octave, "This is you. I've got you!"

Those words, *I've got you*, brought a rush of relief. I wasn't the last person on Earth. He was going to get me out.

I felt him tug on my arm, but I didn't move. *Dude, put your back into it.* He tried again but nothing happened. More voices joined the man and ran over each other.

"Don't move that, you'll crush her."

"That fridge is going to fall right on us."

"Make sure those wires aren't hot."

"She's not going to last long."

I gave them my name. The man's name was John. He told me there had been a bomb. I asked if Northwest Expressway and Rockwell was okay. It was where Donna lived with her five boys, ten miles away. I was imagining bombs from the war movies. In my mind, the bomb dropped from a plane and devastated an entire section of the city. John assured me this was the only place bombed.

I heard the sound of some rubble crash behind me. *Yes,* I thought, *they were going to save me.* The heat and stench felt more intense now, knowing I was about to breathe the fresh morning air. I managed to hook my arm around a thick leather boot. I couldn't feel the texture, but it was sturdy. My right foot discovered something like an electrical cable and I jerked my leg away. I knew nothing about buildings except that power cords carried a deadly voltage. Whatever powered our computers wasn't meant to contact flesh, so I strained my calf to avoid death by electrocution.

Someone on the rescue team mentioned the daycare again. They were confused. One of my work friends dropped off her baby girl every day at the daycare. But the daycare was on the second floor. I was on the third floor. I needed to clarify it.

"Guys…" I started.

"There's another bomb. Everyone needs to get out! Now!"

The call was distant. The sound of shifting rubble stopped. Someone was trying to kill us. I wriggled as I imagined a second bomb falling from the sky. They needed to hurry or we'd all die. "Pull me out," I said.

"Amy, we need to get some hydraulic equipment," John said. "That's the only way to move this stuff. We'll be right back."

I didn't call him a liar. He thought I hadn't heard the warning. The leather boot slipped from my grasp and my arm was left helpless in the empty air. He asked if there was someone he could call. I gave him my husband's name and number. They promised to call and, again, they would be right back in one hot minute. *One hot, explosive, death-dealing minute.*

And then I was alone again. Encased in concrete. Barely able to suck the foul air in a sweltering void. Waiting for a second bomb to kill me.

Images of my life flashed in my mind. Although the words *images* and *flashing* are too thin. You can't describe the Christian cross as simply an *image*. Or say a swastika merely *flashed* across your view. It was more like I saw the tips of translucent icebergs, seeing its surface but also understanding all of its massive dimensions below the waters.

I saw my dad. His stone-heavy frame leaning on the couch, telling me I'd become the bubble blower on *The Lawrence Welk Show*. I'd blamed him for discouraging me, laughing at how futile it was to try become anything more than a housewife. But the image in my mind transformed into something else. It was the same scene, same words, same curl on his lips. But I understood something more, something more true. It wasn't a smirk. His smile had gleamed with pride and confidence. He didn't think I'd fail. He laughed at his bubble blower joke because he knew I had what it took to be more. The only reason I'd failed college was I'd never tried. I could have made it and my dad knew it. But, instead, I'd given up before I ever started. I was the only one to blame for failing.

I saw my mom and her accusatory stare when she inventoried the missing sugar from the pantry. She'd caused my toxic relationship with food. My wild eating in Oklahoma City was caused by the decades of shame and obsession under her keen glare. Her fanatic accounting in her calorie ledger had created the monster in my mind with an insatiable hunger. But, in that moment, I saw something else in her eyes. I saw worry. Fear. I saw her urging me to appreciate a dangerous compulsion inside me. She hadn't been accusing me. She'd been trying to protect me, to warn me. And instead of listening, I'd blamed her. I'd burned the letter and accused the messenger.

I shuddered. Each insight was a darker horror than the heat, the stench, and the distant shrieks of death. I was desperate to get my arm out of the exposed air. I wanted to hug my knees to my chin and rock myself before the explosion ended my life. But I couldn't move. I was frozen in place, my arms open.

I thought of my sisters and all my nephews' birthdays I'd attended. If Donna had a moment to notice me, she'd update me on the latest hour's drama in the house. A fight. A clogged toilet. She'd turn her head to threaten a wooden spoon spanking, then settle back into our talk about daisies. Her exhausted, red-veined eyes were blaring warnings: NEVER HAVE KIDS. But I also thought of her voice when her son got hurt. The way she cooed when she kissed a boo-boo. It rang a bell in my soul, and pained spasms wracked my spine. My diaphragm trembled as I started to hyperventilate, inhaling particles of concrete that sliced my throat. The veil of my willful blindness was stripped by those piercing insights. I saw truth more vividly in that pitch darkness than I'd ever glimpsed from a pew on a cheery Easter morning. And the raw, unfiltered truth terrified me.

I never had a baby. The thought struck me again and again, each time shattering the shreds of my soul into smaller fragments. I'd never held my baby in my arms. Never fed from my breast. Never kissed the tiny cheek after a quiet yawn. I'd missed out on the most primal joy of life for extra cheeseburgers and television reruns.

"Help me." I whimpered. It was too soft for anyone to hear, because it wasn't for any person. I was asking God. I'd lived wrong. I'd indulged in cheap and easy pleasures when joy had been hanging in the air. All around me. All the time. I could have seized it whenever I'd wanted, but I'd squandered the promises of my childhood and blamed everyone else. I'd declined my invitation into the tree of life and jumped into a pit of darkness, all because it was easier to fall than to climb.

"Save me," I whispered. I tried to think about a verse, any verse, to pray. That's what you're supposed to do. There was that verse about life being a vapor that disappears. *How did it go?* I couldn't think of it. All I could remember was that same psalm. *Lord, I walk in the valley of the shadow of death. Please save me.*

Nothing happened. The putrid air stung my eyes as I strained to see any light, any sign of hope. But there was nothing. It was just me in the dark. "I'll change," I promised. "I'll do anything you ask, just save me."

The only response was a distant wail of someone in pain.

"Please," I begged, "I want to have a baby."

This wasn't how it was supposed to go. I'd read the stories and heard the preachers' sermons. When the wayward daughter called, God always answered. I prayed, again and again, telling God I understood now. I got it. I'd lived wrong. I'd rejected joy. I'd refused love. Worst of all, I'd abused myself. I'd cursed and spat on every precious gift God had tried to give. But I'd be different now. I'd change. I'd be better. I'd be the best Christian ever.

But just like my rescuers, God had left me. He didn't know me anymore. I wasn't His daughter. In many ways, I'd never left my back patio in Shreveport. I was still alone, staring into the lifeless dark. It was fitting for me to die in the same way. The stories were all wrong. When you stare into the void, nothing stares back.

My coughs became dry barks. The scratches in my throat burned. The vile heat broiled me. Every breath was like a searing rope being drawn through my nose, roughly forced down my throat, and then strangling my lungs. I couldn't stand another moment wilting away in the dark, waiting for the second bomb to kill me. There was at least one thing I could do for myself. I could at least end the waiting.

I relaxed my right foot and touched the hot wire of lethal voltage.

Nothing happened. I pushed hard on it, and it didn't move. It was just another piece of concrete, or maybe a twisted rebar. Killing myself wasn't going to be that easy. So, I closed my mouth and stopped breathing. A new kind of fire raged in my chest, and I liked it. This was my fire, of my own doing. My head swam and my thoughts started to wander and twist. I wasn't sad. I was glad. Nothing in my life was worth missing. I'd never enjoyed it, anyway. My muscles and tendons twitched. My fat quivered. But I kept my mouth shut. The burning spread into the marrow of my bones. I didn't breathe. I wouldn't breathe. The world would be better without stupid, big, selfish Amy.

AS IT TURNS out, you can't kill yourself by holding your breath. My senses resurged when dust and debris sliced my airways. I was involuntarily gasping. My stomach convulsed as I hacked. I was so completely hopeless and helpless, so weak, I couldn't even kill myself. There was no escaping the second explosion.

In that moment, as my tongue worked like sandpaper to expel bits of concrete, I accepted my fate. I was going to be murdered. There would be no rescue. I would live in torment until the second bomb killed me. This was life. I didn't have anything left in me to fight it.

For some reason, I still don't know why, I decided to spend my final seconds singing. I had no audible voice at first because my throat was too hot and scratched. But my lips formed the words.

I love you, Lord
and I lift my voice,

I didn't think about God saving my life. My life was over. I didn't think He would show up. I just wanted to sing something to Him. Even though He wasn't listening.

To worship You
Oh, my soul, rejoice,

A peace slowly descended upon me, the way a pitched sheet settles softly on a bed. I felt myself turn inward and also outward, toward something that seemed like joy. Like love. Like hope. It felt like God.

Take joy my King
in what You hear,

I thanked God for being God. I thanked Him for giving me everything I'd squandered. I started to blubber. I was so glad He was with me. Here, at the end of my life.

Let it be a sweet, sweet sound
in Your ear.

I sang it again. And again. My throat burned and I sang louder. God still loved me. He had never left. And He wasn't asking anything of me. The heat around me transformed from a strangling rope into His comforting embrace.

For a moment, I thought back to my earlier prayers before. Now that He was here, I told Him I would do anything, everything to experience this holy joy in life. I'd have a baby. If He would lead someone to save me, I would live better. Be better.

He didn't agree to any of my offers. I can't explain how I knew, but I did. He was full of joy, right now, holding me just as I was. He didn't love who I might be in the future. He didn't love my past decisions. He loved me in that moment. He loved stupid, big, selfish Amy. It was unconditional love. Here, seconds before I was about to die, I had everything I'd ever wanted, singing to God as He embraced me.

Then someone touched my hand.

No one had called. Or maybe I hadn't been listening. All I felt was a small tension in my knuckle. I gathered all my strength to squeeze back. I doubt there was any strength left in my hand, but it must have twitched.

"This one's alive!" a man called. "Hurry!"

"Yes, I'm here," I said.

It wasn't the same guy as before. I told him my name. This man said he was Major Allen Hill of Station Eight.

"What's that?" I asked, hearing other voices now.

"We're firefighters, ma'am."

They discussed something in lower tones. Just like the first group, they didn't think I could hear them. They muttered about my position and the amount of concrete piled on. Then one of them said, "There's gotta be a way." And they started working.

"Amy," Allen yelled to me. "I need you to keep talking and tell us if you feel anything."

"I can't feel anything," I explained. "I'm really hot and thirsty."

"We'll try to get to you."

"You'll save me?" I asked.

"Amy, we're going to do our best." I believed him. He wasn't giving me a false hope. But he also wasn't going to give up.

I asked more questions. They explained I was wedged between the slabs of the third and fourth floors, buried under some large pieces of rubble. It looked like I was still in my office chair near the bottom of the pile, upside down.

"Um," I said, "are you saying my butt is in the air?"

"In the chair, ma'am," one said.

My hand wasn't sticking behind me. It was above me. They told me my face was loosely wrapped in a fiberglass curtain, inches from the bottom of the pit. A full refrigerator was dangling above me by its electrical wires.

"Please say my pants are still on."

"Yes, ma'am, there's no moon out yet."

There was nothing sane about my behavior as they cursed and shifted the crumbled blocks of burned concrete. I tried to joke. I cried. I thought I would get free. I thought I was already dead. I don't think anyone can understand the mental attitude or, as strange as it might seem, the dark humor shared in those moments. I still don't understand it myself.

"I'm dying, aren't I?" I'd ask repeatedly.

"No, Amy," Allen would repeat back. "You aren't."

"This is hell."

"It's not that serious, Amy. But, from what I can see..."

I tensed to hear what he'd say. *Was it my leg? Was it already amputated?*

"...you are having a bit of a bad hair day." We all laughed. Belly laughs at the ludicrous joke. Maybe at how inappropriate it was. But, in a way, it was the most appropriate joke to tell. It distracted me from the pit of death.

The work occasionally paused and they'd whisper. I'd say, "It's okay, you can just cut off my leg. I know you need to."

"No, Amy, we're not cutting your leg off."

"Tell me a joke."

"Well," they hesitated.

Uh-oh, I thought. It was my arm. They had to cut off my arm.

"There's another bomb!" a voice echoed.

"Amy, we've got to check on this," Allen said.

"Okay," I said.

"We're coming right back."

"Sure." I knew they wouldn't, but I didn't want to fight them. This had been too good to be true. I wasn't going to live. I didn't deserve it.

"Amy, I swear to you, we're coming right back. We're not going to stop." Their voices drifted.

In seconds, before I could worry, before I could imagine another bomb taking my life, Allen spoke again. "Okay, we're back."

That happened another time or two. During each bomb scare, they ignored the threat and kept working to save me. They risked their lives because they'd promised to not give up. Somehow, they'd find a way to rescue me.

They cussed a lot. Concrete groaned as they heaved away the rubble. Heavy objects crashed. The firemen fell, too. Boots would scrape and a body would grunt.

"Tell me a joke," I said again.

"Well," they hesitated again.

"Is it my leg?"

"No, Amy, it's just," one of them laughed. "We're firefighters. The only jokes we know are dirty ones."

"Well, I'm kinda having a come-to-Jesus moment and that probably wouldn't be right." We laughed some more.

At some point they lowered down a tube supplying oxygen as they edged away the fiberglass curtain from my face. I told them I was thirsty and they lowered a wet rag on a stick. By the time the rag got to me, it was coated with a paste of wet concrete dust. I sucked it dry, anyway.

There was another dull thud and one of the men spewed the most creative combination of curses I've ever heard. "Are you alright?" they whispered to the hurt one.

"If you get me out, I'll owe you all a cup of coffee," I said.

"I'd rather have a beer," one of them answered.

"How about cookies?"

"Sure," one grunted under the strain of something heavy. "Homemade cookies work."

I couldn't bake. I'd have to go to the store and buy the premade cookies. Maybe, for them, I would get the Otis Spunkmeyer tube and actually cook them in the oven. Surely those were better than homemade. I thought about the different kinds. Snickerdoodles were good, but they were basically just like sugar cookies and sugar cookies were too bland. They deserved something more. Oatmeal was more filling, but who wants a healthy cookie? Chocolate chip. Yes, that was the winner. *Wait a second*, I thought, *why am I thinking of cookies?* That's a perfect, big Amy thing to think, in the pit of death. Cookies.

"Deal. You guys get me out of here and I'll make some chocolate chip cookies." They shook my hand on it.

Sometime later, I heard the sound of a saw cutting the back of my office chair. A gray light trickled in front of me and I saw dusted chunks of concrete piled below me. I felt pressure on my hands and body as they wriggled me out. It probably took most of the team to do it. I kept apologizing for being so big as they heaved all of my 355 pounds out of the pit.

They rolled me around on a slab of concrete and I felt blood rush out of my head. The first thing I saw was the stairwell. It was across a chaotic pile of concrete and jutting rebar. I recognized the art that still hung on the wall next to the stairs, an intricately woven Native American quilt. Which meant I was on the first floor. I'd fallen three stories and the heaps of concrete around us were all the floors of the building pancaked on top of each other. *How had I survived?*

I looked over to thank the men for risking so much to save someone as pitiful as myself. I wanted to kiss every dirty cheek. But my compressed numbness disappeared and a train of pain slammed me. I tried to scream, but I couldn't breathe. Someone slipped an oxygen mask around my mouth and I was laid on a stretcher. I noticed I was naked, my clothes mere fragments of soiled fabric. Someone put a medical blanket on me as they lifted me out of the back of the building.

Suddenly, I was looking at the pristine plaza on the south side of the federal building. The street was empty. The façade of the building looked bright and unblemished. It was the same view I'd seen from our routine lunch outings. Full trees and clean benches beneath the rising nine-story building of white concrete. A cool breeze rushed over my face. It was as if nothing had happened. The air was fresh. The stench was gone. The destruction was over. The evil had vanished.

I will never live my life the same, I thought. It was both a statement and a prayer. I had a second chance and I didn't intend to waste it.

A muscular paramedic in the ambulance flicked a syringe as he drew clear liquid from a vial. "When was the last time you had a tetanus shot?" he asked. I freaked out, twitching my body on the gurney, trying to escape the needle. "Girl, you've been stuck up inside that building and you're scared of a shot?"

He eventually put his knee on my chest to administer it. He also gave something to numb parts of my body. As the pain washed into exhaustion, I asked a hundred questions. I kept telling them my husband's name. All the way to the hospital, they placated me. *You're fine. Don't worry about that, now. We've already called your husband.*

They finally gave me a straight answer as we neared the hospital. They told me it was almost four. I counted on my fingers and shook my head. The time couldn't be right. According to my fingers, that meant I'd been buried for over six hours. As soon as I was admitted into Presbyterian Hospital, they sent me to surgery because of some cut on my leg. Right before they carted my bed out of the emergency room for the surgery table, my husband walked in. One look between us, and we connected everything. I felt he understood. We had squandered our lives. We would live differently now. We would choose joy.

But rather than share it, rather than saying something wise and deep about the revelations I'd discovered, I reverted back to my old personality. I made a joke. A bad joke that wasn't funny to anyone. It wasn't even funny to me. As they rolled me into the hallway, I said, "So I guess we aren't closing on our house tomorrow, huh?"

2017 Ironman Arizona

Hour Three

THE CROWDS HOLDING neon poster board signs reading *You're just crazy enough to finish* and *Don't poop your pants* thinned and were replaced by a few gawkers on the city streets. I cycled past houses arranged in neat grids and a few tall palm trees with such tiny palm leaves they looked like Dum Dums with extra-long sticks. After a couple of turns, I was on Beeline Highway heading northeast out of Tempe. The highway was flat and aimed at Red Mountain, one of the oldest mountains surrounding the Phoenix Valley. Or, at least, it was uglier and more deteriorated, like a haphazard pile of muddy laundry. The highway was flanked by a few cacti with thick limbs lifted high, dry spindle bushes, and some kind of larger bush with thousands of thin pale leaves that swayed with an unnatural slowness.

The desert sun started to heat the black asphalt so I took off my arm warmers and tossed them into one of the trash cans at a water stop. I felt good and strong, glancing at my bike computer to check my performance. It was a small digital screen that connected to my gears to track my wattage, speed, and RPMs. I had a good wattage, which meant I was pushing a fair amount of power through the gears. At first, I was glad. That meant the swim hadn't sucked all the energy out of me.

But my speed slowly ticked lower, even with my wattage staying at the same strength. Something was slowing me down. I put my head down to check if my front brakes had shifted to brush across my wheel. It happens sometimes when the bike is jostled hard, but I could still see clear gaps between the brake and my wheel. I thought maybe my bike computer was wrong. But that didn't seem right because I could feel the strength I was pushing through my legs and, after thousands of miles on a bike, I knew what a strong wattage felt like. I was pushing as hard as the computer told me. It was just my speed had dropped.

I looked ahead at Red Mountain on the horizon of the flat highway. Then it dawned on me. This wasn't a flat highway, after all. It was a *false* flat. Our brains often get confused when we head toward a sharp incline in the distance. It twists our perspective, so a slow incline before a sharper incline can be confused as being flat or even downhill. In reality, it's a straight-line incline.

False flats are worse than any hill. With a hill, you can motivate yourself to push up to the top for a minute or so, then enjoy a long moment's rest with the descent on the other side. But with a false flat, there is no rest. No reprieve. You have to hunker down and fight gravity, which feels like someone yanking on a leash around your waist. Even if it's slight tug, the long haul through the false flat burns your legs and eats your energy. The only way to survive the false flat is to suffer through it.

I leaned down on my handlebars and pushed. Occasionally, I'd feel pretty good about my speed. Then a triathlete would pass me. I'd check and see my speed had dropped lower. It was devastating every time, as if I'd cycled two miles forward and was suddenly pulled one mile backwards. The false flat kept me believing I'd made false progress. Each time reality hit, I'd feel the deflating sting of the truth. And then there was nothing else I could do except push again toward Red Mountain.

Chapter Four

Immortal Scars

A FEW WEEKS BEFORE the bombing, the girls and I went to Bricktown to eat a big lunch at Spaghetti Warehouse. Bricktown was a little area east of downtown past the elevated train tracks. Just as it sounds, the restaurant was in a converted big box warehouse with red-and-white checkered tables surrounding a trolley car. I remember that particular lunch because we broke a big rule: we ordered champagne. If Florence ever found out, we would have been in trouble. You can't drink and work with the amount of money we did. It was only one bottle divided among seven girls, so my share of three sips was barely a splash on my mountain of pasta and breadsticks. Still, mostly because we were breaking the rules, I felt as high as a three-margarita happy-hour. I snorted when Sonja told us her oldest daughter finally decided to speak her first words at age three. They had been at a Walmart and she'd screamed a line from a popular TV commercial that resounded off the tile, "Rii-co-llaaaaa!" I will always cherish that lunch. Just a group of girls sharing a secret toast to friendship.

Almost every woman who shared that toast died in the bombing. If life was fair, I would have died and they would have lived. I don't claim those words lightly or as some politically correct script about the deceased. I have pondered the idea for decades and I believe it with my whole being. All of my friends at FECU were better than me. They cared about their work more and tried to help our members more. They loved their husbands more. They enjoyed raising their children. They gave to others with a serving heart in church, charities, or in the small ways they reached out to help me at work. None of them were saints, of course. They all had problems, blemishes, and annoying traits like the rest of us. But, all things considered, their goodness out-matched mine tenfold. They deserved more time to share their goodness and the rest of the world deserved more time to receive it. If life was fair, they would have lived.

But in this life there is evil. And evil is never fair.

THE DOCTORS HAD to perform my leg surgery while I was still awake. Afterward, my sister held my hand but I couldn't feel her. I was paralyzed from the neck down, which the doctors thought might disappear after a few days. They had no case study for a woman trapped upside down for six hours with her entire nervous system squeezed numb between two slabs of concrete, so they couldn't say anything other than, "It will probably pass." Using the word *probably* was a scary diagnosis to hear, but as my mind started to understand my situation, I was more terrified by the images on the television in my hospital room.

Almost fifteen hours after it was first broadcast on the news, I saw the infamous helicopter shot of the collapsed and scorched building. The offices where I'd worked for the last seven years were empty air. The large pile of nine pancaked floors ramped down into the street of upturned cars, shattered glass, insulation, and shredded bits of clothing. White font scrolled the names of 168 people still missing or confirmed dead. I recognized a couple dozen names as my friends at FECU. "Please, let someone find them," I said over and over. I recognized at least a hundred other names as members of FECU. One hundred pleased faces as I cashed their paychecks. *Oh God*, I prayed as details of the daycare emerged, *please save the children.*

I was lucid for only a few hours when a news crew came into my room. They were from *The Today Show* and explained Bryant Gumbel was in town and wanted to do a live interview with me. "Absolutely not," I answered. "I'll only interview with Katie." I don't know why, but nothing mattered more to me in that moment than to interview with Katie Couric. There had been talk in the tabloids of a feud between Katie, Bryant, and the NBC executives over the stories assigned to Katie. Looking back, I'm sure it was nothing more than the normal struggles anyone of any gender has within their organization, but my time at FECU had given me a chip on my shoulder for women empowerment. I had a gut feeling a reporter would want to do my story in the midst of a tragedy. A reporter would want a good rescue story to tell in the aftermath of so much death. The country needed to hear something positive, something other than the endless scrolling of the same 168 names.

The crew told me Katie was still in New York City, so she couldn't interview me. I refused again. I was convinced the NBC executives had chosen to send Bryant to Oklahoma City because he was a man and it ticked me off. It was a silly thing to assume and to project on people I'd never met, but I needed a villain. I'd been blown up and my friends were missing. Children were dead. I was paralyzed from the neck down. And I had no one to blame for any of it. So, I chose to blame an image in my mind of a big boardroom of men in suits trying to keep Katie and women everywhere under their entitled, polished shoes.

The crew finally agreed to make a video interview. They tried to cover some of the hundred tiny cuts on my face, propped up my head with more pillows, and shined bright lights in my eyes. After a time, I heard Katie's voice from a speaker connected to one of the video cameras pointed at my face. I saw her appear on a TV they'd rolled in and I imagined she was glad for a woman in Oklahoma City helping her take a stand. In the interview, she connected me to my savior firefighters of Station Eight. They also spoke through a speaker and I thanked them. The interview ended and I stared back at the TV, desperate for any update on my friends.

Months later, I watched a recording of that day's show. In New York, Katie teased my upcoming interview as a story of hope on the day of tragedy in the heartland. Bryant reported on a roof a few blocks away from the bombing site, explaining the scene was an act of terror and federal authorities were still combing for evidence to find leads for those responsible. In the early morning light, they couldn't tell if anyone was being rescued, but they would keep an eagle eye at ground zero for any updates.

My interview with Katie was alright, from a journalistic perspective. Katie, ever the professional, coaxed me to dive deeper into my emotions of gratitude for survival and appreciation for my rescue. But my responses were brief and slow. In my shock and confusion that morning, my mind combined my first rescuer John with the second rescue team of Station Eight. The confusion dragged the interview into a mix of commingled comments. We ended the segment with me saying "Thank you," and the firemen saying "We're glad you made it out." I hadn't given Katie the Emmy-winning revelation I'd wanted. Instead, even now when I watch the segment, something feels off. It was like we were actors putting on a show while the theatre burned behind us.

I DON'T FEEL BAD about my interview and I doubt Katie feels bad, either. The bombing was unprecedented. At the time, it was the deadliest terrorist attack in the history of our country. We were all trying to find a way to talk about it. In the midst of senseless death, we all tried to find hope. We needed a ray of sunlight to pierce the cloud of evil. We were desperate for our friends to be pulled from the carnage. We wanted the children to be found safe in a closet. But on that day we all learned that you can't force hope into the aftermath of evil. In the midst of trauma and loss, there is only agony and grief.

People like to tell you, "This will pass." They think they are helping when they say, "You survived for a reason." They say these words with good intentions, trying to whisper hope into your grief. But it's the same as the false hope I had for a better future in Oklahoma City. Those words are spoken by well-intentioned friends trying to help because they don't understand their words are lies.

Trauma and loss are like the scar on my shin. I didn't realize how bad my cut was until two days after the bombing. A hydraulic lift creaked as it hoisted all of my 355 pounds out of a medical hot tub with my right leg extended. It was the first time I saw my leg without bandages and I stared in shock. *My bones are gray.* I always thought bones were white, but my flesh was split wide, exposing a shin bone of dirty gray, like the bone on a KFC drumstick. I hollered for the nurses, afraid I was about to bleed out. Of course, nothing was wrong. Leaving it open was part of the healing process.

Over the next several days I recovered the feeling in my legs and arms. The wound on my leg was so large they couldn't stitch it up. I stayed in a wheelchair for a while to let the skin grow back and make sure I didn't damage any of my recovering nervous system. Three hundred and fifty-five pounds is a lot of weight for a spine to carry and the doctors didn't want the compression to cause a relapse of the paralysis. I eventually moved to a walker and, later, could hobble again on my own. It took two months to finish healing from the inside out. But for the rest of my life, my leg was blemished by a deep, blood-red indention running crooked up the length of my shin. In a way, it matched the scar on my soul from my lost friends.

TO MY HORROR, I was one of the last survivors pulled from the rubble. The last survivor was rescued twelve hours after the bomb. For the rest of that terrible night, through the next day, the next evening, and the next night, families huddled around TVs and rescuers searched in vain. For all our prayers, no one else was saved.

While in the hospital, someone figured out another FECU survivor was in the same hall and they wheeled Terri Talley into my room. She reached out and touched my hand while we cried watching the news coverage. For days, we took phone calls from our friends' relatives, asking if we remembered what our friends had worn that day. Like us, their eyes were straining at the pile of rubble, trying to find the color of dress or blouse their beloved wore. Maybe, if they could just find the color on the screen, they could alert the rescuers and save a life.

"I'm so sorry," I'd say. "I have no idea." Besides Sonja's bright yellow suit, I hadn't remembered what anyone wore. The silent disappointment and lost hope on the other end of the line burned me with shame. I could hear their unspoken questions. What kind of friend couldn't remember that simple detail? Didn't I know a life depended on the color?

That kind of shame has never left me. Whenever I think of my friends, a confusing mix of emotions overwhelm my mind and spin until my thoughts are splattered against the walls inside my head. I often start feeling guilt for surviving. I feel a burden of responsibility for re-telling their stories so no one forgets the loss. I feel ashamed for not being friends with every coworker who died that day. Then I feel hesitant to retell any of their stories, friends or not, because they each had people closer to them, who loved them more, who knew them more intimately, and who are more deserving of the honor of telling their stories. Then I feel ashamed again for surviving because I'm reminded of how much more my friends had to give to their families and friends than I had given to mine.

Even today, twenty-five years later, I still don't know how to best honor them when I try to explain what trauma and loss means to me. Maybe there isn't a right way to talk about the deceased. Maybe that's why the loss never leaves us. No matter how hard we try to explain it, no one can understand what the loss meant to us. Every innocence deserves more than a plaque, or a grave, or a memorial, or a song, or a byline. Every death deserves an entire book dedicated to celebrating the beauty of the life. But even then, the book would fall short of the real beauty. Words on a page can never wrap their arms around your neck. You can't have a conversation with a song. A memorial can't warm you with a smile.

I'll never hear what Robbin was about to tell me the moment the explosion killed her and Amber, her seven-month unborn daughter. I can't explain the meaning of beautiful, gorgeous Kathy battling and beating breast cancer, only to die in the bomb with her platinum blonde hair barely regrown past her ears. There's no picture or image that can convey how Karan Shepherd used to make us all laugh into hysteria relating her latest conversation with the swinger neighbors over her fence. No golden memorial can offer me a ride to work the way Christi Jenkins often asked. No number of tears can ask her forgiveness for all the lies I told riding with her, promising I was trying every weekend to get involved back in a church. There is no song, no matter how sweet, that can kiss Sonja's two daughters goodnight.

When their lives were ripped from this world, pieces of our souls were torn away with them. The power of their love is equal to the pain in our wounded souls. And those who remain bear the immortal scars of their love forever.

ONE HUNDRED AND SIXTY-EIGHT people died in the bombing, plus a nurse killed by falling rubble trying to save lives. To put that in perspective, it was estimated that 190,000 people attended funerals over the next month, which was about a fifth of the population of Oklahoma City. A single day inflicted 190,000 immortal scars. Thirty kids lost both their parents in a single moment. Over one hundred of FECU's members were gone. Eighteen of my coworkers at FECU perished. Nineteen children were slain.

There were other numbers, too. Numbers of love and comfort. The term "Oklahoma Standard" was coined to define the acts of selfless giving that flowed in our state, but it was more than Oklahomans. The entire nation rallied behind our city and created a national standard of love and affection in the aftermath of terror. Millions of dollars poured in from California to Maine in supplies, food, water, and loose cash.

Elementary schools drew pictures and wrote messages of love with crayons on giant cards. Stuffed toys were shipped for the orphans to hold.

Donna's husband, Tim, was an attorney and his practice was almost bankrupt after the bombing. He wasn't the only one. Cases were settled or dismissed. Divorces were canceled. Estranged business partners were reunited. Creditors delayed their demands for whatever was owed. The shock of life's true values hit the economy and people let it marinate in their homes and offices. For a few months, people extended warmer handshakes and welcomed hugs over arguments.

There was an American elm tree in the parking lot across the street we used to look at through the conference room window. Its roots were encased in the pavement of the parking lot, but its branches still stretched out far enough for cars to park under the shade of its large green leaves. The power of the blast smashed cars and glass into its trunk, blackening its wood and snapping many of its branches. As the rescue efforts wore on, unknown strangers started to care for the tree. They gave it water and fed the soil with nutrients. Somehow, through their efforts, it survived the summer and in the next spring its branches bloomed with fresh leaves. In the years that followed, it became the symbol for the Oklahoma City Memorial and was named the Survivor Tree.

In a lot of ways, FECU was like the Survivor Tree. The FECU vault was exposed in the blast and no one stole a single dollar. Within hours of the bombing, a meeting was called among the other local credit unions in Oklahoma City. They knew FECU had over fifteen thousand members and now, more than ever, the victims and surviving families would need access to their bank accounts for groceries, gas, and funeral expenses. One of our strongest competitors, Tinker Federal Credit Union, took the lead with selfless giving. They opened up space at their headquarters, converting their teller training room and scrambling to sort through donated computers and printers to create a functioning service center for FECU.

The Teachers Federal Credit Union, the ESEO Federal Credit Union, and the Oklahoma Educators Credit Union loaned employees to run the teller line and work the back-office systems. Fort Knox Federal Credit Union operated on the same computer programs and systems as FECU. They paid travel, lodging, food, and salaries for six employees to fly into Oklahoma City to help the service center get running. In just 48 hours after the bomb, competitors and total strangers had FECU running again to provide essential transactions for all our members.

None of their sacrifices was about publicity. None of the credit unions advertised to the public about their giving heart or asked for money back to recoup their losses. They were driven by original mission of all credit unions, the motto of "People Helping People." Credit unions are run by a volunteer, unpaid board of directors guiding their operations. The immediate response by the local credit unions on the day of the bomb was the most natural action for them to take. The board and all the employees were obsessed with delivering every cent of revenue right back to the people. A lifetime of selfless giving had sharpened our skills and forced us to keep flat, agile organizations that could move a mountain with one shovel and a few hours' notice. And the little, rag-tag community of credit unions saved FECU.

MY WINDOW IN Presbyterian Hospital overlooked Lincoln Boulevard, the road leading through the state government's buildings. Back then, every car had headlights you had to manually flip on and off. A newspaper had suggested for Oklahomans to drive during the day with their lights on to show support for everyone who had survived or lost someone. I'd stare out my window as the sun washed over the busy street and see every car with its headlights still on, some of them flashing their brights as they passed the hospital. It sounds like a silly gesture, but it meant everything to me. I felt the love of the city beaming into my room with the morning light and whisper, "His mercies are new every morning."

When I was told the hospital would release me in a wheelchair, I wondered what home I'd go to. "Our new one," my husband said.

"But where's our furniture?" I asked, "We don't even have a bed."

"All taken care of." He explained his coworkers had moved our furniture. The largest store in town, Mathis Brothers, donated a mattress and delivered it for free. A local church spent a Saturday digging postholes, erecting our backyard fence, and laying fresh sod. Our new house had been ready for a week.

On my final day in the hospital, I got a visit from a large man wearing a cut-off jean jacket with a snake tattoo curling around his bicep. "Do you know who I am?" he asked with a gruff voice.

I'd never seen the man before. His bald head and bushy beard made him look like a member of an outlaw biker gang. But I recognized his voice. "Yes," I said, "I do."

Two days before the bombing, one of our tellers had received a furious phone call from a man I dubbed Mr. Jerk Face (except I actually called him something more scathing). He was going through a divorce and wanted us to shut off his wife's access to their joint bank account. Obviously, because it was held jointly, we couldn't do that unless she also signed off. The teller transferred the call to me because Mr. Jerk Face was belligerent. I explained our policy and the the law on joint bank accounts. He spat, "Honey, let me talk to the *man* in charge."

He didn't know the *man* in charge was Florence Rogers, who would have no problem ripping a new hole in his ear. I told Mr. Jerk Face, "*She's* not in, but I'd be sure to give *her* the message." He cursed me with some choice words and hung up. I never gave Florence the message.

Now Mr. Jerk Face was standing in my room with wet cheeks. He put a single red rose on the foot of my bed and choked out two words, "I'm sorry."

He left the room and I tried to call after him, "I'm sorry, too."

THEY CALL IT the new normal. That's how psychologists and therapists talk about immortal scars. They know loss and trauma are added to the definition of your life forever. Their focus is to help you accept its permanent change to your perspective of life, like a gray filter laid over your soul, dimming your light. The counselors help you adjust to your darkened life until you can discern the colors again. Like a woman who has lost a leg, she has to learn to maneuver in life with a cane. She can live fully again, but only after she's accepted her leg is never coming back.

My new normal took years to accept. I'd be in the food court at the mall and see a man eating alone. If he glanced at me, I froze in terror, absolutely convinced the man was about to pull out a gun to shoot me. Every time a speaker squawked from a rock song played too loud and especially when jets roared from a low airplane, my head would spin as if I was falling three stories. The flashbacks felt so real the horrible stench underneath the rubble would sting my nostrils. Just the thought of walking back into the office made my legs tremble and my forehead trickle cold sweat. Every start of a project paralyzed my mind with the haunting faces of my dead friends that used to help with those projects. I often excused myself to the bathroom so I could stifle my sobs alone in the stall.

With my counselors, I learned about trauma, post-traumatic stress syndrome, and grief. At least, I learned those were the medical terms for my raging hormones, disabling depression, and blinding anxiety. When I'd been rolled into surgery those first moments in the hospital, a nurse had leaned over and whispered in my ear, "You need to talk about what happened to you. It's the only way you'll heal." The counselors encouraged me to keep repeating my sensations and feelings being trapped and my grief from the loss of my friends. Connecting my spiraling thoughts to their medical terms helped me organize and understand my emotions. It was like a big net I could use to collect my swirling emotions and then sort into separate buckets. An airplane might set my mind and body into a new torrent of anxiety, but as I worked with the counselors it got easier and quicker to collect and separate my thoughts, feelings, and physical reactions.

By the end of May, I was able to work a couple of hours a day at FECU. Florence Rogers had survived the bomb. At 9 a.m., she'd been talking about our financials with all the department heads in her office. In a flash, Florence was alone, laying on the carpet, inches away from the empty space where the eight managers of FECU had fallen to their deaths.

Florence drove us back to work as soon as possible. She cornered us at funeral services to insist we return. At the time, we were angry and upset with her insistence. But, looking back, I can see she was offering us healing. If she could distract our minds back at work, we could start moving on. The more time we spent working without our friends, the quicker we'd build new memories in our new workspaces with new colleagues. She sacrificed her own grieving to offer us a faster path to our new normal. By June, I was working half days and in July I was back full time, leaning on a walker to relieve the pressure from my scarred leg.

IT TOOK ME eight months to build up the courage to deliver the cookies I'd promised to my saviors: Allen Hill, Chris Thompson, Mike Roberts, and Vernon Simpson. It's hard to describe why it took so long. Part of me was afraid seeing them would ignite a new anxiety attack. But it was also like the fear of meeting the eye of someone who gave you something truly amazing. If you've ever been poor and had someone give you that extra $100 to make your rent payment or borrow a car to drive to an interview, then you know what I mean. Meeting their eyes feels rude because you feel like you aren't their equal. Now imagine someone saved your life, risking their own lives through multiple bomb scares and with a massive fridge three stories above threatening to rip free and smash their skulls. I was entirely unworthy of their presence, to meet their eye, or to give them a hug. Handing over cookies seemed like an insult compared to their sacrifice.

Just as I'd imagined when I was buried under the rubble, I went to the supermarket and bought a blue plastic tube of Otis Spunkmeyer chocolate chip cookie dough. I fumbled around with the oven, put on my best outfit, which was black to make me seem thinner, and drove to Station Eight. A reporter came to record the meeting for a piece about the firefighters and the whole city's gratitude for their work.

The men were all smiles and love. They chomped on the cookies and told me they tasted better than beer. "You deserve more for hoisting me out of that hole," I joked. "It was just your luck to find the big girl."

"Yes, Amy," Allen Hill said, wiping crumbs from his mustache. "We were the lucky ones that day. We got to save someone." I kept my grin but the guys looked earnest. "Most of our friends didn't get the chance to help anyone. We were blessed to find your hand."

MY HUSBAND and I tried out a few churches on Sunday mornings. My experience with God under the rubble gnawed at me, telling me to reconnect more intimately with a Christian community. But I couldn't make it through a service without my anxiety and grief overwhelming me. Every sanctuary, every pastor with a suit reminded me the funerals of my friends.

I had vivid dreams at night. I'd be on an airplane near the window and a black storm would rock us. Lightning would strike near the engine, the lights would flash, and a woman would scream. Or I'd be in my living room watching TV with my husband. The wind would howl and a tornado would rip the roof off our house. I'd feel myself falling into another pit of a thousand speakers throbbing with bass and wake up unable to breathe, my sheets drenched in my sweat.

My counselor said my dreams indicated I still couldn't accept what happened to me. She said my mind was still convinced a natural force had caused the tragedy and I needed to accept that a man had intentionally chosen to inflict evil on me. She told me to find something outside the office to help me process, cope, and accept my new reality. My *new normal*. With my Christian upbringing, I'd always believed in good. Good values, good deeds, and good people. But I'd never accepted evil. A man could spend his weekends volunteering at a soup kitchen feeding hungry mothers, or he could spend his life savings constructing a fertilizer bomb to kill infants and strangers. The contrast between the beauty and goodness of my friends and the dark horror of Timothy McVeigh was too stark. It was a chasm wider than the Grand Canyon and I couldn't build a mental bridge long enough to connect the two. I couldn't accept both realities existed in the same world.

My oldest brother Mike gave me a Martha Stewart gardening book while I was in the hospital. One night after an especially bad dream, I read through it, front to back. As I read, I'd hear in my mind Martha's almost comically gentle voice, but in those dark nights her voice soothed me. Reading about soil pH levels and ways to prune a rose bush focused my mind on something beautiful. By the next spring, I had my first garden mapped in my mind and, almost without thinking about it, each stage in my garden was dedicated to one of my fallen friends.

For Robbin, I planted purple iris. They had complicated layers of purple petals that looked as if they were peeling away to reveal something magical inside. Kim got windflowers because minutes before the bombing she'd told me hers had started to bloom. I planted pink azaleas for Kathy because we'd argued once about how hard or easy they were to grow. Claudette got the daffodils she'd always asked me to get from my mom's garden.

I had a hard time figuring something for Sonja. There were lots of options I considered, like roses, daises, or orange tiger lilies, but none of them fit into the flowers and staging I'd already chosen. Good gardeners are like fashion designers. The aesthetics of the entire plot had to be considered. It's never as easy as simply adding a different flower. Exchanging one color changes five other placements across the bed. One day I was at a bookstore flipping through a gardening magazine and I caught Sonja's name in large letters. I knew in an instant I'd found her flower. It matched her personality perfectly and I wouldn't need to shift anything around. I completed my garden with bold, bright, and cheery Sonja sunflowers, matching her final, grand laugh moments before the bomb.

Planting and nurturing the garden became my new therapy. Witnessing the shoots rise and buds bloom into the spring sun felt like a kind of resurrection of my friends. Like they had all sent me a small drop of heaven. Every time a bud blossomed, its delicate petals seemed to brush away another cloud of darkness from my mind.

A LOT HAS BEEN said about Timothy McVeigh and I don't care to repeat most of it. A federal trial was held in Denver and the prosecution team wanted me to give a testimony. It was two years after the bombing but I still had anxiety attacks leading to it. I would wake up two to three times a night in a hot sweat, sometimes screaming. I wanted to call the prosecutors a dozen times to cancel, but I knew my friends deserved better. I would force myself to sit in the witness box and watch a video from one of our office parties to describe the lives of my fallen friends. When I arrived in Denver, the prosecutors informed me I wouldn't testify, after all. The judge had ruled my testimony would be too prejudicial, a lawyer term meaning it was too emotional. I thought the ruling was ridiculous because blind murder is nothing but emotional.

Instead, I sat in the courtroom next to the mother of Paul Ice, a DEA agent killed in the bombing. The back of McVeigh's shaved head drew my gaze like a black hole, as if my soul was being sucked into his void of evil. When I finally forced myself to peel my eyes away, I did a double take at the bailiffs. They were some of my original members at FECU. Seeing them gave me comfort. Even though we were hundreds of miles away from Oklahoma City and in the presence of McVeigh, this was still home court.

After the trial, McVeigh would give a detailed confession to reporters on how he'd planned the whole thing and considered the loss of life as collateral damage in his war against the federal government. The dead children meant nothing to him. For everyone sitting in the courtroom for his trial, that confession was no surprise. McVeigh smirked through the whole ordeal. He basked in the attention and the drama. He seemed to enjoy seeing his plans posted to the evidence board and the scenes of terror he'd created. He was a man who'd chosen a dark path and was too afraid to glimpse back toward the light and consider maybe he'd made a wrong turn.

A decade later I learned to forgive Terry Nichols, one of McVeigh's accomplices who helped build the bomb in the Ryder truck. I could forgive him because he apologized for the pain he'd caused, even if it was intentional. But I could never forgive McVeigh. I don't know how to forgive someone who continued to boast about his evil to his dying breath.

The jury found McVeigh guilty. The prosecution refused all media and, instead, met with the survivors and victims' families in the basement of the Holy Ghost Catholic Church, two blocks from the courthouse. It was a beautiful church with cream bricks and medieval archways. Bottles of uncorked champagne in gold ice buckets were waiting for us. It was the first alcohol I'd sipped since our secret toast to friendship in Spaghetti Warehouse. There, in the basement of a church with lawyers and priests, it felt like my friends were with me as we toasted to justice.

I had a new dream after the trial. I was in the passenger seat of a truck and Sonja was driving. We were downtown, going the wrong way up a street. Somehow, though, I knew there was a bomb planted behind us that was about to explode.

"Step on it!" I screamed to Sonja. Even though a flood of cars were coming toward us, crashing into those cars was better than being blown up. I stretched my leg across to step on the gas for her, "Go, go, go!"

"Congratulations," my therapist said when I told her about the dream. "You've finally accepted the bomb was an act of man."

ACCEPTING THE BROKEN nature of our world is maybe the most difficult phase of healing from trauma and loss. The unfairness of nature's impartial cruelty and humanity's intentional acts of evil are tough realities to accept. Before the bombing, I'd spent a lifetime avoiding those harsh truths. Like when I flipped through the channels during the Waco incident where agents, women, and children had died—that level of pain and suffering didn't seem real to me. I watched movies to feel the emotion of loss without really believing it existed. I thought *Die Hard*'s explosions looked cool without thinking of how a building blast would actually feel.

I still believe that, if life was fair, I should have died and my friends should have lived. They call that kind of thinking *survivor's guilt*, but that sounds like I'm shaming myself. It's not shaming if it's the truth. You see, immortal scars aren't shameful, unfortunate, or unnecessary. Immortal scars are markers of the day we discovered one of life's hard realities. It's the day we lost our innocence, or maybe just our ignorance, and learned the reality of pain and suffering in the world. That's why I don't like it when someone describes survival as *recovery*. Survivors never recover the person they were before the loss and trauma. For the rest of our lives, we think of our past in two phases: the person we were before the event, and the person we became after.

That's also why I don't like the term *accepting your new normal*. I think the best way to describe survival is accepting the *real* normal. The hard, ugly realities have always been present. We've just ignored them. We bubbled ourselves away from hurt and pain, away from sickness and hunger. But no matter how hard we try, or how much we eat, or how much we justify buying wi-fi connected appliances, life will always find a way to hurt us. Nature's disasters and humanity's evil slay the good and the bad unfairly. Sooner or later, somebody will offend you and there is nothing you can do to prevent that. Sooner or later, your beloved will die, your friend will fall into addiction, or your mom will get sick. There's nothing good about the day pain and suffering finally strike, but there's also nothing abnormal about it.

Every April, when I'm quicker to fly into an anxiety attack or sob from a memory of a friend, I use breathing techniques to calm my heart. I try to avoid airplanes and schedule lots of time at home with people I love. I don't consider any of my tics or emotions abnormal. I accept the broken world along with my emotional and physical reactions to it. I believe we become survivors the day we realize immortal scars are the most natural and inevitable condition of humanity.

But there's more to life than surviving.

There is something that can defy the unfairness of evil. There's an ability you can learn to overcome your immortal scars. You'll never be protected from suffering, pain, and heartache, but you can pierce through those storms with the light of hope burning inside you. And the day you learn to practice hope, you stop being a survivor and start your transformation into someone new.

Part Two

CHAMPION

2017 Ironman Arizona

Hour Five

I NEVER REACHED Red Mountain. It loomed at the horizon of the uphill highway, retaining the same size in the warming desert sun no matter how far I pedaled. There was a simple cone in the highway with volunteers in neon shirts screaming "Turn around ahead!" The course was three laps of the challenging false flat followed by an exhilarating downhill ride back into the city. With gravity reversing and my power piston thighs churning, I practically flew down the hill.

Back into Tempe, the course narrowed with the fans cheering behind barricades of advertisements for Gatorade and body glides. I saw my husband waving his hands and screaming something at me. My trainer was close, too. "They're dropping like flies," I heard her yell. I gave her a thumbs up. The miles were going fast and I felt good. A little tired, but that was expected. I flipped around another cone and headed back into the desert.

This time my speed dropped even lower than my first lap even though my computer showed I was giving the same wattage. Something was very wrong now. I did all my initial checks again on the little computer, my wires, and listened for a brake that may have shifted into the wheel. Everything seemed fine. I passed by a skinny dude crouched low on his bike, like a turtle with his head tucked into his shell. That's when I noticed some flags flying outside the last green patch of farmland before the long climb toward Red Mountain.

It's called a straight flag day, which means the wind is so strong the flag is almost stiff in its right-angled, picture-perfect rectangle. On the first lap, the false flat had felt like I was dragging a baby seal. Now, with the wind careening uninterrupted down the long highway, it felt like the seal's mother was slamming her tail into my chest. I had to clench tight on the drops of my handlebars to keep my balance and I saw a few cyclists headed the opposite way with nasty road rashes down their calves.

It finally occurred to me what my trainer had meant. She wasn't talking about the *miles*. She had meant the *athletes* were dropping like flies. And, actually, I was pretty sure I saw Ruth and Chris standing next to her when she'd said it. They hadn't made the swim and other athletes were starting to fall behind on their time. The false flat and the wind had set themselves against us, and we were losing.

I lowered my head, trying to shrink my chest so I'd become more aerodynamic. I drew up to another cyclist struggling. "We didn't train for this!" the cyclist shouted without looking at me, either unable or too afraid to shift his head in my direction.

Actually, I had trained for this. I hired a coach with six months left in my training. I knew the value of a mentor, but it had just taken me some time to find the right match. Most trainers were obsessed with getting their athletes onto the podium. They'd charge into the gym with trails of fire behind them, punching fists in the air and slapping a high five every two minutes. But I wasn't trying to place. I just wanted to finish. Being an Ironman, by itself, would be enough.

"You mean Iron*woman*," one athlete corrected me, giving me this weird smirk and nod like we were members of a secret society. I knew the type. I met women like this in conventions and chamber meetings across the county. They mean well. Heck, I'm the girl with a pink bike, pink jersey, pink sunglasses, and pink helmet. I know a thing or two about female empowerment. But changing the Ironman name for a woman finisher cheapened it. It's like telling someone you qualified for the Olympics in running and having them correct you by saying, "You mean the *women's* Olympics."

"No," I said. "There's only one Ironman and I'm going to be one."

My coach, Erin, understood me. When I told her I only wanted to finish the day and nothing else, she nodded and said absolutely. "Even if you're the last athlete to cross that finish line, Mike is going to call you an Ironman."

Still, she pushed me as if I was trying to finish first. If I missed a swim, she called me until I answered. When I uploaded a long bike ride, she e-mailed me wondering why I'd taken so many breaks or why I didn't power up the last hills. I'd make an excuse, like my leg hurt or my heart rate was getting too high. Then she would analyze my heart rate zones and convince me that my body had more to give. Under her guidance, I broke some of my long-standing physical barriers and mental blocks to reveal an entirely new trove of strength in me.

So, when the desert gods raged, I was ready. I took a deep breath, shifted into a lower gear, and started to spin. I knew I could do it because Erin had shown me how. I could hear her voice in my ear, telling me I was strong. Telling me I needed to dig deep because victory doesn't come easy. Telling me to keep pushing if I wanted to be an Ironman.

And then there was the other thing.

I was an Okie. I'd been forged on sweltering summer roads and in winters of black ice. I'd cycled in winds that broke the stems off wheat and kept a falcon gliding for an hour without beating his wings. I'd lived through tornadoes and if an entire building couldn't keep me buried, this wind didn't stand a chance.

Chapter Five

Kindling

HOPE IS A VERB. It's not a wish or a destination. It's not the distant star in the night sky. Hope is the jet fuel that propels you to the moon. Hope's true meaning and power is *you* have the ability to change *your* future. You, and only you, can create a better company. You, and only you, can lose your weight. You, and only you, can run a marathon, fix your marriage, retire early, get a degree, or start a family. Hope is the force that drives you to change. Hope is the phoenix fire that burns away the past and gives birth to something new. You, and only you, can ignite hope in your life.

Hope is a verb.

In a world where unfair and unjust evil looms, hope is both fair and just. Hope is a force inside you that can fight back against the world's infliction of pain, hardship, trauma, loss, shame, prejudice, and abuse. No matter your genetics, your parents, your culture, your spouse, your children, your work, your boss, your friends, or any other force in your environment that tries to push you into despair, nothing can stop your hope. You, and only you, can enact hope anytime and in any area of your life. You always have the power to push back the dark.

Lots of research has been done on hope. Believe it or not, there are scientific ways to measure and predict the level of hope a person contains, and how that hope will impact their future. In the lessons of my life, I learned hope is a verb with four steps:

1. Take an honest assessment of yourself and your world.

2. Set a goal.

3. Map a path to your goal.

4. Take the next action, no matter how small, toward your goal.

It sounds easy, but practicing hope is hard. Of all those steps, sometimes the first step of hope is the most difficult. Or, at least, it's the step that hurts the most. For me, it took the loss and trauma of the bombing to take an honest assessment of myself and my world. I wish no one had to face death to discover they had wasted their life. I wish no one had to suffer the agony of grief to understand the reality of this broken world. But, all too often, it takes the searing knife of tragedy for someone to take an honest assessment.

It's not always that bad. Across the country, people have told me their stories of deciding to live with intention before death knocked. From Mississippi to Florida to Oregon to Maine, I've met women and men ready to get honest with themselves about what they've wasted while chasing the suburban fantasy of security and comfort. They decide to risk stepping outside their picket fences before death knocks on their door or heartache strikes inside their bug-sprayed yards and security systems. Please, if there's anything you can learn from the first phase of my life, don't wait. Don't waste the short time we have in life wallowing in your own dark pit of willful blindness. It's never too late to start. Today, take a look at your life and take your first step in hope.

AS YOU MIGHT IMAGINE, FECU was all but destroyed from the

bombing. We had no office, no computers, and no vault. Most of our management team and half the staff died. The surviving employees were bruised, scattered, maimed, and emotionally scarred. The easiest thing to do, which many suggested, was to merge with another credit union in order to survive. Small credit unions like ours frequently merged when they struggled. Given our organization had been reduced to literal and figurative rubble, the technical obstacles to merge would have been easier to surmount than rebuilding. But Florence and the FECU board wouldn't do it. Instead, they made it their mission to show the world we could survive, rebuild, and thrive in the aftermath of terror. And if we could do it, so could the rest of Oklahoma City.

With the downfall of the banks from the '80s oil bust, there were plenty of empty office spaces built for financial institutions available. We chose something in a historic suburban neighborhood in the northwest part of the city. At least, relatively historic in Oklahoma City's one hundred years. Bethany was a town split down the middle by Route 66 and, as the interstates turned Route 66 into a memory, Bethany was swallowed whole by the rest of Oklahoma City's vast expansion. It was most popular in the 1960s and 1970s as hosting The Strip. You know, the street in most cities teenagers cruise up and down in their new cars on Saturday nights like in the movie *American Graffiti*. Tinker Federal Credit Union had recently shut down a branch on The Strip and they offered us the space at a discount. It was already built to handle a credit union's operations, from tellers to loan officers to the back office, vault and all. We simply turned on the lights and opened for business.

A year after the bombing, FECU was fully staffed and growing thanks to Florence's unrelenting drive to keep us moving. Rather than allowing us to limp into work to lick our wounds, she had the audacity to push us to grow. She cupped our chins and forced us to look up from the gravestones, toward her vision of a better future. She'd turned on the first lights as the first tenant in the Alfred P. Murrah Federal Building. She'd built a team and an organization that grew from almost nothing to fifteen thousand members. She would not let FECU, or any of us that survived, rest until we were firmly planted back where she'd begun. One year after the bombing, she succeeded. We opened up our first satellite branch, our logo posted once again on a downtown building. A year after that, Florence announced her retirement. Her battle was won, her race finished, and it was finally time for her to rest.

The board promoted a new CEO and within a few months some of the deep problems of our credit union started to stunt our progress, mostly because we made it extremely hard for the leadership to accomplish anything productive. Have you ever heard someone at a funeral criticize the deceased? Or, worse yet, explain to the mourning crowd how the deceased should have been better? Of course not. When someone passes, you remember and cherish the fond memories. You choose to forget anything other than the best.

In an organization, that mentality is a problem. An organization must change. Repeatedly. And often. But any new change that was suggested carried the unspoken inference that someone who had been killed didn't manage the right way. The survivor employees didn't like it. We didn't intentionally destroy progress for that reason, but subconsciously we had our reservations and it kept momentum from building. We were so emotionally nostalgic from the sheer trauma of the bombing that we worked hard, intentionally or not, to preserve the past ways. We were obsessed with keeping the status quo.

There were other problems, too. Every manager was either a new employee or, like me, promoted by default for being the last employee standing in the department. With an entire new management team with no mentorship or hand-off, almost every issue became a power grab. Instead of working as a team with a common purpose, we often resorted to acting like a collection of individuals with our own agendas. And, more often than not, our agenda was some justification to prevent change.

In other words, our credit union refused to take the first step in hope. We resisted taking an honest assessment of our need to make sweeping organizational changes because we were too scared of disrupting our past.

I LEARNED my first lessons in hope from my first mentor. Vicky Texter had been the head of our credit card department. She was one of the managers that died falling from Florence's office on the morning of the bombing. Two years before that, I was promoted from the teller line to be her clerk. The entire credit card department consisted of Vicky and me, which made me something like her glorified secretary, but I still called it a promotion because it had a tiny bump in pay. I cried when she'd told me I had the job because I was so grateful and also ashamed to know I'd been her absolute last pick. I'd applied for the job multiple times over the years and Vicky had never even interviewed me. Instead, she'd picked anyone else, even a pregnant girl we all knew would never come back to work from maternity leave. I think she may have been forced to take me because there was no one else applying.

Rather than treat me as her last choice, Vicky invested all her effort as if I'd been her first. She slowly gave me more tasks to manage and refused to accept any of my normal playbook of excuses like having a dumb brain. If I got something wrong, she forced me to do it again and again until I got it right. She invited me to attend the loan department staff meetings, where they played cassette tapes of personal motivation speakers like Mary Kay. According to science, Mary Kay explained, it was impossible for a bumblebee to fly. Its body was too heavy and its wings too thin. And, yet, it flew.

Unlike beautiful blonde Kathy, Vicky looked a lot like me: a plain face, big-boned body, and hairstyle that looked more like the *Before* picture in magazine advertisements. But none of that mattered to her. She didn't have to be pretty, thin, or styled to make a big difference in the credit union. She single-handedly created the credit card department from nothing. No one had suspected back then how big credit cards would become and with few resources she kept up with the growing transactions and quickly changing laws.

It was my job as Vicky's clerk to post payments and prepare credit card applications. At first, I'd tried my old manipulative games.

"This payment won't post." I mentioned one day when the system wasn't working right.

"What should we do?" Vicky asked.

"I've never done this before," I said. When Vicky didn't respond, I continued, "I have, like, no idea."

"How would you figure it out?"

"By asking you."

"If you have questions, the manual is right there," she pointed to our bookshelf and I pulled down a three-inch manual about Visa payment processing. Two hours later, I figured it out.

It would have been so much easier for Vicky to simply bark an order to her clerk. She could have treated me like the girl I kept telling her that I was: big, dumb, uninspired Amy. But she refused to accept that version of myself. Instead, even if she didn't see it, she chose to speak to an intelligent, driven woman somewhere inside me. Over time, my insecurities evaporated and I discovered something impossible: I wasn't hopeless after all.

Maybe a month before the bombing, I tried an experiment. I'd been taking mental notes on how Vicky might be figuring the credit limits she approved on the applications I'd prepared. I wrote on a Post-It note the credit limit I thought Vicky would give the applicant. Without a word, Vicky handed me back the application later that afternoon with the identical number written in ink for the approved credit limit.

A week later, Vicky told me she was leaving FECU. She said it was time for her to go. She'd lost seventy-five pounds over the past year on her Subway lunch diet—five years before they'd started their Subway Diet marketing campaign. She said she'd outgrown our small credit card department and needed a new challenge.

"You should apply for my job after I announce it," she said.

I laughed. "No way," I said. I still counted on my fingers and couldn't imagine managing the program by myself. I wasn't smart enough. Or pretty enough. Or assertive enough. Or witty enough. Or strong enough.

Two days before the bombing, I found a card on my desk. The front of the card was a painting of a dense forest. It wasn't a dark, lonely forest like my nights in Shreveport. This forest had brightly colored birds swooping between lush branches and diving into a crystal stream. Inside the card was a single sentence in Vicky's handwriting:

The woods would be very silent if no birds sang except those that sang best.

Vicky's funeral was different than any other. They called it a *celebration of life*. They played upbeat music. People clapped and shared stories that filled the room with laughter. I should have been sad and weeping, pondering the meaning of life when a woman as good as Vicky, who lost seventy-five pounds and was weeks away from leaving FECU, died in a senseless attack. But I couldn't keep from smiling at the rich joy of her lovely family and friends celebrating her life.

Even in death, Vicky was teaching me something about how to live. Rather than looking at the sadness and grief, she wanted to inspire the moment to celebrate life. Rather than considering all the ways I was dumb and useless, she wanted to inspire me to consider how I might learn and help in any situation. She flipped my perspective of my life from a long list of failures to a limitless list of opportunities. She guided my first steps toward intentional action and revealed a bit of hope inside me.

It was Vicky's lessons that allowed me to notice the problems at FECU after the bombing. I got honest with myself about my contribution to the toxic work culture and recognized big changes were needed. Vicky had shown me there was a way to change myself, and I suspected the same process was true for an institution. Even though I wasn't smart or educated, I felt like her card was her dying prayer for my life. I may not have the prettiest voice in the forest, but I would still sing.

"IF YOU COULD wave a magic wand to change anything, what would it be?"

I was sitting in our CFO's office about a year after Florence retired. I'd started having morning chats with Lynette because she reminded me of Vicky. She had short brown hair with stud earrings of real diamonds. Her office was at the end of the hall where no one ventured and I enjoyed learning a few bits of wisdom every week talking about the struggles of our credit union.

That particular morning she surprised me with her fantasy question and I was even more surprised at how quickly I blurted out some sweeping organizational changes. It was easy for me to talk about them while we sat in her room away from anyone else. I had fun with my fantasy wand, like I was conjuring up my very own credit union. I invented new incentives programs to reverse the negative energy. I shifted managers and reworked teams to create a better environment that might actually get something done. After probably fifteen minutes, I realized Lynette hadn't said a word. I got nervous that maybe I'd gone too far and added, "But, of course, I wouldn't know any better. And it wouldn't work, anyway."

Lynette answered softly, "Amy, you are the future of this credit union. The people who are going to lead this organization aren't at the top right now. They are one layer down."

I walked out of her office bewildered. What I didn't know was Lynette had just turned in her notice to the board of directors to quit. In her letter, Lynette explained she had wanted to help change the credit union for the better as CFO, but she'd failed. She'd spent the hour that morning with me making sure someone in the credit union understood the same issues she saw. It was like her version of leaving a note in her desk for the incoming officer to read.

The next morning there was a commotion at work. The chairman of our board was standing outside our CEO's office. He announced the CEO would be leaving employment and Lynette was our new CEO. Lynette walked into the lobby and I saw something incredible. From her first words, she took charge of the entire company.

"I know you're all worried right now," she announced, tugging her jacket tight to her waist. "But if you're here to be a team player and do your best every day, you have nothing to worry about. We're going to trim the fat. Then we're going to do something great."

Without hesitating, Lynette blew through the hard decisions as easily as she blew the steam off her morning coffee. She promoted the people willing to work without politicking or excuses. She had high expectations of performance and made sure everyone was clear, always, whether they met her standard or were falling behind. It made us all jump when she asked, but also feel satisfied when she paid a compliment. In less than a month, we were all moving forward together and she'd gained the respect of the team. It was like Lynette really did have a magic wand and she'd waved it to make our credit union blossom. It felt like we had a new purpose that wasn't mere survival. We were a part of a grand vision for a better future.

It felt like hope.

For some reason, Lynette took me under her wing. She often came into my office or called me into hers to talk about an issue like implementing time cards or a management reorganization. I always gave her my honest opinion, even when I was scared to disagree with her thoughts. We'd talk out the issue and she'd settle her mind on a direction. As she explained to me, she enjoyed that I wasn't a "yes man" in the organization, with the courage to voice an opinion, no matter who it might rub the wrong way. I don't know why she picked me to mentor. I often felt like I had nothing to offer. But as the credit union grew and flourished, Lynette promoted me to Vice President of Operations.

A YEAR AFTER the McVeigh verdict, I got pregnant. The absence of children was my most potent regret while buried under the rubble and we tried for some time. When I finally saw those blue lines on my pee stick, my hope swelled. But in December of 1998, we lost the baby in an emotional miscarriage. I laid in bed in darkness for a week, feeling helpless and buried all over again. I felt an unbearable shame, certain the miscarriage happened because I was so big. I'd filled my body with so much unhealthy energy there was no room for joy. My husband kept a steady pepper of jokes between my bouts of depression and we started to try again. In December of 1999, one year after my devasting miscarriage, we gave birth to my son, Austin.

Just like the grief from my immortal scars, I can't describe the beauty of birthing a child into this world. It would be easier to draw a picture of our infinite universe or count the blades of grass in my yard. When I held Austin, his small mouth touched my skin and his breath tickled my neck. My past life, with all the darkness and grief, felt cleansed and renewed into something as pure as the white around his big blue eyes. Occasionally, a wild thought crossed my mind: *If I'd never been buried, Austin would have never been born.* It was a shocking thought. It didn't make me thankful for the bomb. Nothing could. But it was a true fact that jumped in my brain and re-crossed itself in a way that made me dizzy when I kissed Austin's puffy cheek.

Back at home, I realized there was nothing pure or cleansed about me. I had no idea why Austin would cry or why he would stop. Donna laughed at me and stayed a few nights to show me some tricks. It was like messing with the printer back on the teller line, fumbling over switches without a clue. If Austin was hungry, why wouldn't he latch on to me? Why did I have to tilt him three degrees to the right and face Egypt to make him sleep?

Four weeks after giving birth, I went back to work. I convinced myself Lynette and the rest of the credit union needed me. The truth was they'd made arrangements and I could have stayed at home. I thought giving birth would make me become more like Donna. I wanted to be like those perfect moms, happy and content to spend my day rocking Austin and laughing when he spit down my shirt. But I wasn't. I loved Austin with my whole heart, but I didn't love staying at home all day. I was bored and the new home life of stepping on rattles and washing dirty bottle nipples made me feel dull.

If I was a man, people would have understood and agreed. "You've got to get away from the house to stay sane," they'd say at the coffee pot. But as a mother, I wasn't supposed to admit that I preferred my forty hours at the office over staying at home. To me, work was the only area in my life where I had some kind of control. My office desk was the only place I felt the warmth of hope.

2017 Ironman Arizona

Hour Nine

IT TOOK ME more than seven hours to make the three cycling laps toward Red Mountain and back. The cacti stopped looking like cheering fans with their arms up and more like giant green hands raising a middle finger. The false flat and wind sucked the energy out of my thighs as I powered through my last trip into the heart of Tempe. I was finishing this leg of the triathlon a little slower than I'd wanted, but I still had hours to spare before the next cut-off. Getting a DNF on the bike course was never a fear for me. Cycling is my superpower. What I feared came next.

The legend says as soon as the first man completed the first marathon in ancient Greece, his heart stopped and he fell over dead from the exertion. Now, tired and exhausted, having already exercised for nine straight hours, I was about to start my 26.2-mile run. And I had to do it with a busted knee.

Over the last year, an unbearable pain had developed in my knee. At age 50, it seemed my knees had finally had enough. My years of abuse from being overweight had pummeled my cartilage into paper-thin shreds. A couple months before the Ironman, the pain was so bad I could barely run a mile without limping in pain. So, with Erin's help, we devised a strategy. I found a medical center with a treadmill pool to do a few ten-mile runs. The pool buoyed my weight, so I could still exercise my running muscles on the moving treadmill at the bottom. A week before the Ironman, I got cortisone shots in my knees. It was a temporary fix to keep my bones from grinding long enough to make it through the triathlon weekend. But, still, I knew my muscles weren't in marathon shape and, ready or not, it was time to do it.

I coasted my bike through the barricades into the last transition area. A volunteer took my bike, thank God, because I was about to tip over as I unclipped my shoes. I hobbled into a tent that blocked the late afternoon sun and downed some shots of pickle juice to help with my muscle cramps.

"You're doing so well!" Erin shouted. She helped me exchange my cycling shoes with running shoes and stuff packs of ice into my bra to cool off. "There are so many dropping out. That wind is crazy."

I nodded and stuffed an Uncrustable in my mouth. It was no longer cool and the peanut butter oil oozed down my wrist. "How much time do I have?" I asked. It was simple math. Everyone knew the final cut-off was midnight and my watch showed it was almost five. But my brain was numb and I couldn't figure it out.

"You've got about seven hours," she smiled. "That's a pace of about sixteen minutes a mile. Think you're up to that?"

I tried to think encouraging thoughts. Years ago, I'd completed a marathon faster than seven hours. But I had good knees then. And I hadn't swam 2.4 miles and biked over one hundred miles first. To keep positive, I imagined what I'd look like crossing the finish line before midnight. I imagined hearing Mike Reilly's voice calling me an Ironman.

"There's always hope," I said. Erin helped me to my feet. Out of the tent, Terry leaned over the gate and gave me a kiss on my salty cheek. Then I was off.

Cycling works some of the same muscles as running, but the circling motion is very different than the linear motion of running. When your thighs have been circling for seven hours, it takes them some time to understand your new instructions to push straight forward. With the added problem of fatigue from a seven-hour bike ride, running takes an intentional concentration for every stride, with an amount of effort that seems unbelievable to move your relatively lightweight feet. In other words, it feels like your feet have turned into heavy bricks.

I was relieved the cortisone shots had worked. As I started to trot down the course, my knee didn't hurt at all. It was the first time in over a year I didn't feel any pressure or tinge of sharp pain. I clicked the run start on my Garmin watch and ran up alongside a guy in his 50s. We ran together at a healthy pace. When I checked my Garmin again, I was surprised. I was running a pace of an eleven-minute mile and I wasn't even pushing myself yet.

My coach's plan had worked. I was running at a pace five minutes faster than I needed. That meant I'd cross the finish line with two hours to spare. Mike was going to call my name. I would raise both fists in the air and let out a primal yell of conquest. I'd survived the swim. I was a natural on the bike. And now the power of hope would carry me through the run.

Chapter Six

The Fire

ALMOST TEN YEARS after the bombing, people called my story incredible. I was 38 years old and, without a college degree, I was a vice president of a financial institution. Our growing credit union had built a new headquarters and opened a few additional branches. Austin old enough to pour his own cereal and use the remote to find his cartoons. We had finally found a church that didn't make me cry. It was picture perfect to everyone, including myself.

My contentment felt real and rich. It was nothing like the empty comfort and false security I'd chased before the bombing. In less than ten years after the bomb, I'd achieved everything I'd wanted. There was no place higher for me to go. I was a mother, an executive, and actively engaged in a church community. My joy kept me smiling through the days and sleeping soundly at night. I started getting invitations to speak about my story at small, local women's groups. Every time I spoke, the women would comment on my recovery as an inspiration. They told me I'd totally transformed my life, and I agreed.

"Just try it," Lynette urged me, "you'll be surprised." She was insisting I do something called a *painted picture*, where you close your eyes and write out a description of your perfect future. Just like Vicky had used the bumblebee lessons from Mary Kay before the bombing, Lynette encouraged our team to learn and practice personal development tools.

"Oh, believe me," I said, "I've done this before." I refrained from explaining to Lynette for the umpteenth time that I'd done a version of goal-setting when I was buried in rubble. I may not have written the words, but I'd had my fair share of envisioning a better future.

"Do it again."

"But I've accomplished all of it. There's nothing more for me to do."

Lynette rolled her eyes. "Why do you come to work?"

"To get paid," I shot back. She smiled and leaned forward, clearly not letting me off easy. I sighed and added, "Because there's a bunch of stuff to do."

"Will we ever be finished growing our credit union?"

"Of course not."

"Well," she said, spreading her arms, "the same goes for your life."

I'd never thought of my personal life like that. I never considered that my life, like my work, should never be finished.

Lynette continued, "Of all people, you understand we only get one chance at life, and we owe it to ourselves to keep trying. So, please, write something."

You can decline an invitation from your boss once. Maybe twice. But when she urges a third time, it's no longer a request. So I closed my eyes.

"Imagine your perfect life in the future," Lynette said. "Forget about the past and forget about today. If you could write the perfect ending to the movie of your life, what would it be?"

I thought and then wrote down something about Austin going to college and being happy. "That's all I've got," I said.

"Remember the magic wand?" she asked. I smiled, remembering our talk the day before she became the CEO. "What could a magic wand do to your marriage? Your spirituality?"

I closed my eyes again and wrote some details about my marriage improving and getting closer to God.

"Now, what do you look like?" Lynette asked.

I wrote out some details of my own life. I wrote about being thin and fit. In the scene I described, I was passing beautiful flowers and trees on a bicycle. "Okay, this is getting weird," I said. "I haven't been on a bike since I lived in Shreveport."

"Maybe you should buy one."

"Yeah, I guess so." I clicked my pen and handed her my paper, feeling good. I wasn't going to buy a bike. The tires would pop if I hopped on any bicycle with my 355-pound body.

Lynette pushed the paper back to me. "We aren't done yet." She told me to imagine my career. "In the fairy tale of your life, what kind of job do you have? Who have you become?"

I rolled my eyes and put my pen back to the paper. I thought about being a fashion designer, making clothes for big women. I imagined myself winning the lottery, flashing cash at the fancy tailored stores in 50 Penn Place. I thought about working in a gardening center. My pen made some scratches on the paper and I opened my eyes. "Uh oh," I said. At the bottom of the page I'd written three letters: C.E.O.

"I'm not sure I want that," I said.

"You wrote it," Lynette said. "And it doesn't surprise me. Remember what I said to you that day? You are the future of this credit union."

It took me months to accept it. I thought Lynette had used some kind of dark magic to make me write about bicycles and being CEO. Maybe there was an inaudible, subliminal track playing from behind her desk. But the more I thought about it, it didn't feel so weird. It felt natural, like an old memory. I thought about my time buried under the building and the thoughts that flashed through my mind. I'd thought about being better in my career. Maybe my dream didn't end as a vice president.

"Well," I told Lynette one morning passing by her office, "even though I don't know how, I'm going to prepare for it. I'm gunning for your job."

"Take a seat," Lynette pointed inside her office to her two purple cushioned chairs. "And shut the door."

The purple chairs. They were side-by-side in her office, with a strategically placed table the exact size of a box of Kleenex between them. Whenever a purple chair talk happened, that Kleenex was used.

My chair groaned as I eased my body's weight on it. Before Lynette could settle, I quickly started to talk. "I'm sorry. I shouldn't joke like that," I said quickly.

"Maybe," Lynette said, "but that's not what I want to talk about. You see," Lynette sighed and looked out her window. "You need to understand the world is changing. I made CEO because I had the experience and skills. But these days, boards need to see more from their chief executives. They want an education on the resume." She half-closed her eyes, "I will be the last CEO of this credit union without a degree."

It felt like Lynette had just pulled on my arm to help me half-way out of my chair, only to drop me. My heart plopped deeper into the plush cushion than my heavy body. She had planted the idea of being CEO in my head to begin with, and now she was back-tracking. Of course, I'd never be a CEO. I was stupid to even consider it. The painted picture was a pure fantasy. The business spreadsheets and financial statements were the truth, reserved for the smart people of the world like Lynette. No one would hire a CEO who counted on her fingers to calculate the tip at Chili's.

"But you can get a degree," Lynette said. I nodded and left, pretending to consider enrolling back in college.

There was no way I'd try it. People already wondered how I'd become a vice president with no education. I'd kept my two failed semesters in Shreveport a secret. Not even Lynette knew. If I enrolled in college now, I'd fail and everyone *would* know. They'd replace me at some point. Maybe not Lynette, but the next CEO would. No one would trust an executive in a financial institution who couldn't pass basic math courses. There was too much to risk and, even if I risked it, I was too dumb to pass any of the classes. Heck, there was no way I'd even get accepted into a college. No way. No how. It was, in a word, impossible.

There's gotta be a way.

The words of my rescuers echoed in my mind. It was impossible for me to get a degree, sure. Then again, it had been impossible for me to survive the bombing. But my rescuers saved me, anyway. They had looked at the mountain of concrete pancaked on me and the industrial fridge hanging by a cord above them and said "There's gotta be a way." They ignored the bomb threats and risked their own lives in their hope of saving mine from the clutches of an impossible situation.

So, maybe if I just tried, there was a way to achieve the impossible.

The next morning, I ducked my head into Lynette's office. "I'm going back to college."

"That's great," she rang.

"But it won't look good if your vice president has a degree and you don't," I said. "So I think you should enroll with me."

Lynette looked at me like I was a charging bull. It took her a few moments to relax her eyes before she said, "Fine. Find us a program and I'll join you."

THERE IS NOTHING TAME about hope. Hope is a wildfire that, once ignited in one area of your life, can spread and burn into others. After witnessing hope's power in my years at work, Lynette convinced me to apply hope to my personal life. The painted picture exercise unveiled goals in my life that had been dormant for decades. It was a new way to take those first two steps of hope: taking an honest assessment of my life and setting a new goal. It would have been so much more comfortable and secure to continue being a vice president until I retired. Trying to become CEO meant trying new things and risking failure. There were all kinds of ways for me to screw it up. But after building up hope through work, I felt empowered to tackle something in another area of my life.

I didn't know how to even start, so I worked through the third step of hope: mapping my path towards my goal. Getting a degree seemed too big of a jump. It was too daunting. I couldn't envision what that path looked like.

"How do you swallow an elephant?" Lynette would often say in our work meetings. We all knew the answer: *one bite at a time*. If any step in my path seemed too daunting, I just needed to break it down into even smaller steps until there was one thing I could do today to bring me closer to my goal, no matter how small. I pulled out an index card and wrote: *Get a College Degree*. Then I made a list of smaller steps on the back. To get a degree I needed to pass my classes. To pass my classes, I needed to study a certain number of hours each month. I also needed to attend the classes, which meant I needed an evening or weekend school program. To enroll in that program, I needed to pick a college. To pick a college, I needed to research my options.

I wrote out all the steps and, satisfied with the day, I put the card away. I spent a couple more days building up the courage and then I took the first, small step of searching. It was easy to look up options online, so it didn't take long for me to start. I didn't want a degree from one of the fly-by-night schools popping up around the country. I was getting a degree so board members wouldn't doubt my credentials to become CEO. If someone perceived my diploma as coming from a fake university, that seemed worse than having no diploma at all.

I settled on Southern Nazarene University. They had an evening program designed specifically for working adults. It wasn't any Harvard, but it had a brick and mortar campus and a basketball team with a pretty impressive history. The Nazarenes were considered an extremely conservative denomination in the Bible Belt, but they weren't completely stuck in the patriarchy of the past. Donna had attended and received a theology degree.

The next step was to call the university to schedule a meeting with an enrollment advisor, but I couldn't bring myself to dial the number. I felt paralyzed all over again. The creeping expectation of a better future brought potent memories of danger and death. Once before, I'd felt the thrill of starting a new journey and then my life shattered to pieces. I'd moved to Oklahoma City searching for a brighter future and instead I'd gained weight and had my concept of marital bliss shattered. My only sustaining joy had been my friendships at work, and they'd been destroyed in an instant. Now, as the anxious excitement of a new journey started to build, I felt like failing was inevitable and everything I cherished would perish.

I tried talking to Donna for some encouragement. She'd gone back to school and survived while raising five kids. But then again, she'd always been smart. She'd done well in her classes in Shreveport before marriage. Plus, her husband was an attorney and they made a ton of money. For me, the cost of the program was too high. We still struggled with credit cards and car loan payments. And when would I have time to study? I'd never studied in my life. It was like telling a fish to fly. Three years of doing something called *studying* and shouldering a massive heap of debt was too much. I didn't have the brains to pass the first test or the money to pay for the first semester.

"It feels like I'm jumping off a cliff," I told Donna on the phone. "I can't really prepare for it because I have no way to gauge how much effort it will take. I going to fall with no parachute."

"You are," Donna agreed. Then she added, "But sometimes in life you have to jump first and build your wings on the way down."

So, I jumped without wings. I called the number and made an appointment.

"None of your credits will transfer," the advisor told me. She was maybe ten years younger than me with bright berry lipstick. Her wall had three diplomas framed in a kind of velvet red wood with cursive words I couldn't read. Unlike me, she'd lived right the first time. She hadn't put a boyfriend above her studies. She hadn't dropped out to spend her nights staring into the dark. She didn't need to count on her fingers to calculate my transcript from Shreveport with a 0.5 GPA would not be accepted by a legitimate university.

"You just aren't qualified for admission."

"I know," I said quickly. No future fantasy could erase my past. Maybe no amount of hope was enough. Maybe you couldn't swallow an elephant. I'd have to tell Lynette that, sorry, I was too dumb for school after all. She'd hire a new VP of Operations and I'd have to find a job where I didn't have to count money. "Thank you, anyway," I said as I hoisted myself out of the chair.

"Hold on," the girl said, motioning me to sit back down. "Don't worry, I've got ya." She clicked her nails on her keyboard and printed out a few pages. If I passed a few classes in a local community college, she could use those credits as proof of my ability to get admitted.

So, I took my next small step. I applied to a smaller program and was accepted. I swapped my evening television shows for studying. Before I knew it, I'd completed fifteen credit hours, clearing classes like *Intro to Essay Writing* and *Health and Wellness*, surprised I could pass a health test drinking a sweet tea and eating a candy bar.

I went back to the advisor with my new rap sheet of a 4.0 GPA for fifteen hours. "Great," the advisor said, "but I still can't admit you." Apparently, proving my worth only qualified me for a bridge program, a kind of high-intensity training program designed to help working professionals gear up for the actual degree program. I felt defeated yet again, but I was getting used to that feeling. Every time I got knocked down, I took a long shower at home and woke the next morning focused on taking the next step in my impossible journey. At work, I pulled out my index card and added *Finish the Bridge Program*. Six months later, I finished the program and was accepted into the organizational leadership degree program.

Then, of course, I had to still pay for everything. I'd written on an index card *Find a Butt-Load of Money*. The cost of college was a higher obstacle than my time spent studying. It would take penny-pinching for two years to pay for just one semester. On the back of the index card I wrote *Ask Mom for Money, Get Lots of Loans, Apply to FECU for Tuition Assistance,* and *Win the Lottery.* I struck them all out as I completed them. Except the lottery, of course. I'm still waiting to hit a jackpot.

I DIDN'T HAVE the courage on my own to get through college. That much was obvious from my first two tries in Shreveport. I could do the actions of hope like taking an honest assessment, making my goal to get the degree, and even writing out the small steps it would take on the back of index cards. But when it came to summoning the courage to take the next action, I was empty. I didn't have the courage or willpower in me, on my own, to do it. So, without realizing it, I developed a little trick. I didn't have a name for my strategy back then, but today I call it being trapped into courage.

I like to compare hope to a fire because practicing hope burns. It may not be a searing flame charring your skin, but it takes a bit of suffering to enact hope. It hurts emotionally to take an honest assessment and it sure feels like pain to turn off Netflix to study books. It can feel like total agony to finish work on a grueling Monday, only to drive straight to college for a four-hour lecture on profit and loss statements. It takes courage to choose the transformative fire of hope.

My most courageous moment was when I was buried under the rubble of the bombing. My rescuers were having trouble freeing my leg, and time was short because we were all afraid the building might collapse on us. I was so desperate to escape, I kept telling my rescuers to cut my leg off. In the moment, I was confident losing a leg was a better option than losing my life. I preferred the pain of amputation over the pain of death. I was full of courage, but when I was finally pulled free and laying in the ambulance, I was terrified at the sight of the needle for my tetanus shot. I lost all my courage the moment I was pulled free from my pit of death.

In a way, that's why I invited Lynette to join me. I knew the long years with lots of studying and lectures would be hard. I would suffer and feel that special kind of pain every time I cracked open the sticky pages of a new textbook. And without something more dangerous at risk, I'd never do it. So, if I added the risk of my boss watching me fail in the same program, I knew I'd be motivated to pass every class. If missing one class or failing one test jeopardized my career, I was far more likely to show up and study. The pain of disappointing my mentor and boss far outweighed the pain of studying. I trapped myself to find the courage to endure the next step toward my goal.

THE PROGRAM put us through one course every five weeks. We met in the same room every Monday evening from six to ten. I was relieved the room was tables with office chairs that didn't have armrests. I would have never fit in the traditional desk-chairs made for the kids fresh from high school. The professors changed with the courses and they'd lecture, highlight sections of the books to study, force some discussions, and assign group projects.

Lynette was with me the whole way, even in the bridge program. One of our first classes was math, and I discovered every meaning of the word *study*. With Lynette sitting next to me, failure wasn't an option. I tested myself on the equations for hours at home and even at work. When the class ended, I slapped my A grade on Lynette's desk and finally confessed my greatest secret. Yes, I'd taken this class before. Yes, I'd failed twice. Yes, I was smarter than I thought.

I gained a few more successful grades before we started one of the easier classes on the schedule: *Intro to Christianity*. Every degree at Southern Nazarene University required one purely Christian class, and I was glad for the break from studying Excel formulas and marketing philosophies. Having grown up in church and with a husband with a Bible degree, I eased into the seat next to Lynette, ready to pass this class with my eyes half-closed.

"Amy Downs," the professor started our session in front of me. "Do you have a sister?"

"Yeah, Donna McCoy," I answered with a forced smile. I had been afraid of this. Donna was a genius and had surely impressed a professor or two while she'd attended here. Back in high school, this happened all the time with my older brother, Alan. He had graduated valedictorian five years before me and I had to witness each of my teachers make the slow, agonizing discovery that I was nowhere near his level of intelligence. Whatever hope I had to coast through this class withered in a moment.

"Mm-hmm," the professor said. Her eyes didn't light up and she paid no compliment to Donna. She walked back to the front of the class without speaking to the other students. She seemed annoyed. I exchanged a confused look with Lynette. No, it wasn't annoyance. It was something else.

"What did you do to this woman?" I finally asked Donna on the phone after an especially odd interaction I had with the professor a few weeks later.

"Oh," Donna finally gasped. "I am so sorry, but it's actually *your* fault." Donna had enrolled in the theology program at SNU in the mid-'90s before the bombing. There was only one other female in her class trying to get the same degree: my professor. We'll call her Kate. The environment from the men was tense toward Donna and Kate. Once, a couple of guys blocked Donna in the break room to demand she quote a scripture giving women permission to study theology. She escaped only by pressing her whole body into one of their arms to squeeze out of the doorway. Donna and Kate quickly learned to sit together in the corner, fighting together in class discussions against an all too often belligerent patriarchy.

A few days after the bombing, the students huddled around Donna to hear her explain the story of my survival. At the end of her story, Donna concluded, "The doctors said it was a miracle she survived."

"How dare you," Kate said. "God doesn't do miracles." For two hours, the debate raged in the class. Some agreed with Donna that God could perform miracles. Others claimed God never intervened. To them, God having the power to save me meant God chose not to save my friends. "If God saved your sister, then God killed those children," Kate seethed. Donna and Kate were never friendly again.

I relayed Donna's story to Lynette while we sat on her purple chairs with the door shut. "What do you think?" Lynette asked.

"I don't know," I said. "Yes, I call it a miracle sometimes. It's all I can say. But some days, it feels like I only survived because I'm so big, my fat saved me."

"Well," Lynette said, putting her hand on my arm, "I believe it is absolutely a miracle."

I didn't want to argue the point with my boss, so I just nodded. I couldn't explain that I also believed God should have saved my friends over me. And especially the children. I would never make sense of surviving in the wake of the blind evil that day.

"I don't mean surviving," Lynette continued. "No one can understand that."

"Then what?"

"The miracle is the person you've become after that day."

THE COLLEGE PROGRAM was only three years long because we went through the summer and winter, with just a few weeks skipped for the major holidays. As I continued passing my classes next to Lynette, she gave me more responsibility at work. It was fun to take concepts we just learned in school and apply them to a personnel problem or management tactic. Often, it worked. At the end of the program, my grades made me eligible for *magna cum laude* status and the other working adults voted me as *Most Outstanding Student*. I donned the large black gown with an extra-special tassel on my cap. Almost twenty years after I'd flunked out of college, I walked across the platform to the cheers of my family and friends. I saw Lynette, draped in black herself, touch the corner of her eye with a Kleenex.

"This thing is empty," I laughed with Donna. The leather portfolio I'd been handed had fine print explaining my real diploma would be mailed to me after I finished paying my final balance with the school bursar. It would take me a while because I had more student loans than car loans now. "What a racket!"

"At least it's finally over," Donna said.

"Oh, I'm not finished yet," I said. "I'm going to get my master's."

2017 Ironman Arizona

Hour Ten

WE RAN alongside Tempe Lake where we'd begun ten hours earlier. Now the sun had crossed the sky and was setting in the west. The grass next to the lake was so lush next to the dirt path it looked like a neon putting green. The air cooled and I kept checking my pace on my Garmin watch, every time amazed at how well I was performing. I even chatted with the guy running next to me around the three-mile mark.

"You can do it!" someone shouted from the street, "Just one foot in front of the other."

"Oh, *that's* how you do it?" I shot back. It was probably rude to demotivate someone trying to encourage me, but I was tired and I meant it in good spirits. I was cruising to the end of my impossible race.

"I heard this joke the other day," the guy next to me said, "there was a cyclist coming down a mountain when he stopped to let a goat pass. The goat belted out just three--"

I stopped running. The guy glanced backwards but ran ahead. I tried to start running again and my legs barely moved. I walked for a few minutes, occasionally starting to run, only to immediately stop again. It wasn't just the feeling of my legs like bricks. If anything, my legs felt numb. I just couldn't get them to run again. I had to lean my body forward and force my feet to move, if only to catch me from falling on my face.

I recognized someone ahead of me. His name was Glenn and he could be spotted from a mile away with the tattoos that covered his body. He'd completed multiple Ironman triathlons over the years. I'd talked with him a few times on the group runs and rides in Oklahoma. He would be able to help me. "Glenn," I called as I forced myself to stumble near him, "What is this?"

Glenn looked at me with a stone face, then turned his head back to the road.

I called after him again, "Am I going to be alright?"

He said nothing. My feet tripped up and I barely caught myself. Glenn kept running without a second glance.

With twenty-three miles left to run, I could barely walk.

Chapter Seven

Shedding

I TOOK Austin to the Oklahoma State Fair in the fall of 2007. The fairgrounds sprawled over a hundred acres just west of downtown, with small buildings filled with animals, rodeos, and booths of homespun clothing and crafts. The weather cooled in September but you could always count on a healthy dose of rain to ruin whatever day you'd planned. This year, though, the clouds stayed thin and we were free to enjoy the fair's main attraction: food.

Every foodie knows the state fair offers the best splurge meals like corn dogs, Indian tacos, and chocolate-coated cheesecake on a stick. Every morsel is soaked in the subtle flavor of aged oil from grease pits uncleansed for decades. I showed Austin how to eat funnel cake without inhaling the powdered sugar into his lungs and we both tried the year's newest attraction, the deep-fried Oreo. The flaky crust of sugar was drizzled with fudge sauce and the warm center melted in our mouths. I felt heavier than ever walking around the carnival row, like a ten-pound block was resting in my stomach. The carnies shouted louder when they spotted Austin next to me, promising large, fluffy tigers and bears for a one-dollar game.

"It's not true," I tried to explain to Austin. He tugged on my loose pant leg and started to whine, as if he'd die without a stuffed tiger. "They promise it's easy to win, but you'll end up being disappointed." Of course, it was useless to explain the tricks of marketing to a nine-year-old. I only had a few dollars left in my purse and I wanted something sweet to drink after all the salty food.

"They're doing it," Austin pointed at a young family tossing rings on a bed of glass bottles.

"But we're smarter than that," I said. I let him watch the family try three more times and fail. The parents tried to laugh it off but their daughter looked heartbroken to walk away without the mermaid doll she'd been eyeing.

The sun was setting as we walked through the rest of the carnival toward the exit. I felt proud. Austin had learned something today. I'd given him his first lesson in the temptations of false promises.

"I want to do that!" Austin squealed. Near the exit was a small ride, if you could call four red buckets with a string of lights a ride. The buckets twirled around on mechanical arms, lifting and dropping in jerky movements.

"We'll never get on that," I said.

"Please, please, please," he asked with the sweetest eyes. I should have stayed firm, but sometimes a mom wants to spoil her son.

We waited maybe ten minutes in line. The teenage attendant with acne and thin hair explained in a monotone voice that Austin wasn't tall enough to ride by himself so I had to ride with him. It took all my dollar bills and a few moments of counting quarters from my purse to pay. The metal groaned when I stepped onto the bucket, squeezing myself into the door and pushing Austin into the sidewall. The attendant dropped the safety bar into my thighs. "Ma'am," he said, "this needs to go down."

I shifted my legs apart and sucked in my tummy to try creating more space.

"Mom, you're squishing me," Austin said. I told him to hush.

The teenager tried again, but the bar barely moved. "You'll have to step out."

"What?" Austin asked.

"Ma'am," the attendant lifted the bar, "if the safety bar can't engage, you can't ride."

"It's okay," I said, "I can hold him."

"Ma'am," the teenager gestured for me to get off.

"What's he saying?" Austin asked. The other riders looked at us impatiently.

I leaned toward the teenager. "Can he stay?"

"He's not tall enough," the teenager said with his monotone voice.

"Why can't we ride?" Austin asked.

"Please," I begged.

"Ma'am, you're holding up the ride."

The metal arm creaked and bounced when I stepped off. Austin started to cry with fat tears. I glanced at the line of people waiting and saw twenty faces quickly jerk away from me. Austin pulled on my arm back toward the ride, screaming, "No! I want to ride. I want to ride!" I had to practically carry him all the way to the fair exit and he kept wailing in our car. I shifted my rearview mirror so he couldn't see my mascara streak down my cheeks.

That evening I ate an entire box of Lucky Charms after dinner. I'd finish a bowl with a little leftover milk and pour some cereal to mop up the milk. Then I'd run out of milk and, because I didn't want to eat dry cereal, I'd pour in a little more milk. And so it went. *In the morning,* I promised myself as I hoisted into bed. *In the morning I'll start my diet. Austin will never cry over my weight again.*

The next day, as I thought about how embarrassing the scene at the fair had been, I ate a candy bar before lunch and had a steak finger meal from Sonic with a huge coke. Diet Coke, of course. *Oh well,* I thought. *Monday I'll start for real. Starting on a Sunday was silly, anyway.*

On Monday morning my stomach rumbled as I rolled into the Braum's drive-through. "Hold on a second," I called to the speaker box, "I'm ordering for someone else, too." I settled on two sausage, egg, and cheese biscuits with two hash browns, a Diet Coke, and a coffee. I drank the Diet Coke and ate both biscuit sandwiches and both hash browns in the car before I got to work, leaving the coffee untouched in my console. I walked straight to the office bathroom to brush off the crumbs and grease that had dripped on my chest. *The first day of October*, I told myself. *The first day of October, I'll start my diet. Starting in the middle of the month was silly, anyway.*

FOR TWENTY YEARS, I'd been living for the next morning, the next Monday, or the next month. The shame of two decades of failed diets, lost exercise plans, and broken promises weighed heavier on me than my 355 pounds. Every day, I'd wish my life was different. I'd wish I'd never gained my weight, that I could easily slide by someone when we crossed in the hall, or that I didn't have to think about a chair's strength before I sat in it. Every day, I'd convince myself tomorrow would be better. Tomorrow, I'd change. Tomorrow, I'd lose the fat trolls clinging to my bones.

And, every day, I'd blow it. I'd eat the donut. Every day, my stomach would rumble and I'd chomp hamburgers, fries, and cookies. I'd order a chocolate shake after lunch. A candy bar or two for an afternoon pick-me-up. Oreos smashed in ice cream after dinner. *Tomorrow*, I'd promise when I'd finished binging. *Tomorrow, I'll be different.*

It is as simple and as complicated as forgetting. When the urge to eat triggered, I'd forget everything except food's promise to make me feel good. The urge was like a lightning bolt in the center of my brain, splintering to shock every nerve of my spine, organs, and skin. The world stayed the same but everything inside me shifted. I couldn't think about the report on my screen, remember who to invite to lunch, or consider anything I'd promised myself yesterday because every brain cell was firing with memories of rich lo mein or buttercream frosting. The pleasure of the memories, by themselves, had such potency my mouth watered and my stomach growled. Nothing else mattered except to feel that sensation again.

If, by some chance, any other thought found its way through the superstorm of desire raging in my brain, the thought would instantly be rain-wrapped into the storm and become part of it. If I thought about health, I'd instantly realize I was a bigger girl who burned more calories to carry my weight, so I needed to eat more calories, too. If I thought of refraining from sugar, I'd remember I was a career girl who needed the mental energy bump to get through the next project. On occasion, I'd remember my promise the day before. On occasion, I'd say to myself, *No, not again. I won't do it.* The storm would quiet and I'd feel like I'd won. In five minutes, the storm would rage again and I'd forget the victory I'd just experienced. Every cell in my body, every mental faculty, and every physical motion was driven toward consuming food.

When I wiped my mouth, the storm clouds cleared and my destruction was laid bare in full light. I was fooled again into consuming a full city of calories. I believed the lie of cheap pleasure and, alone, I felt shame. It was like the family I'd seen at the state fair. The carnie twirled the strands of his mustache as he pocketed the money. The pristine, beautiful mermaid remained untouched, hanging in the stall, and another layer of shame was added to the twenty-year pile on my soul.

No one can bear that much shame. For all my talk and experience with hope, I shied away from an honest assessment about my weight because twenty years of ten thousand failures can't be reckoned. The only way for me to get up from the table after an embarrassing meal and back to work was to tuck the shame away. I learned to do this quickly. I'd move through my day without thinking of my weight or my broken promises. I'd do anything possible to ignore the cold truth of my crushed will and huge body. I'd try to forget who I really was.

Tucking away the truth created an extreme dissociation from my body. When I walked near bay windows next to buildings, I'd see the giant reflection of my body and think, *That's not me.* I couldn't see

115

anything of myself in the waddling mass in the window and I'd look away. Rather than take an honest look and try to reconcile what I saw, I refused to accept the image. I'd walk into the shower without looking at the mirror and be glad it was shrouded in the steamed mist when I got out. Blue and black stretch marks clawed across my stomach and waist in twisting streaks like surface veins with sickened blood. I couldn't accept them as part of me. None of my flesh looked like me. I would not accept it.

WHEN I LIVED in Shreveport, I'd thought DD was the largest size of breasts, reserved for the Pamela Anderson creations of plastic surgeons. I didn't know the scale could go further, all the way to my JJ breasts. Oprah unveiled a new bra one year that looked like a cross between a corset and a medieval torture device, with lace and hooks intersecting wired frames and stiff plastic. But, oh my word, those bras worked. I could almost hear my back give an audible sigh of relief after I'd holstered myself in.

The only store with clothes my size was called Catherine's. It was run by a large black woman (although still skinnier than me) who had empathy for the plight of big-women fashion. I'd roam the aisles of blouses, pants, and slit skirts. Eventually, I'd end up at the same rack at the back of the store. Even here, there was a limited set of options for women of my size. All of the dress suits were Sunday church clothes and each came with a matching hat. Nothing in these sections was bright and certainly nothing flesh-toned. There were no available sizes larger than mine. If I gained any more weight, there would be no place in Oklahoma City to buy new clothes.

Group meals were scary for me. When you have JJ breasts, you can't see the ground and restaurant floors are rife with potential slick hazards. It's easy to fall when three degrees of leaning adds a hundred extra pounds on one leg. Getting up is even harder and I was terrified of becoming a beached whale on the floor of the restaurant. If I didn't have to ride with anyone, I'd race to the restaurant at least fifteen minutes early so I could ask for a table. If someone got there first and seated us at a booth, I'd be doomed. Sliding into the booth made the table stab my stomach and, again, my JJ breasts would hunker over or, worse, rest on top of the table. The others would quickly look away, everyone too embarrassed to ask for a different table.

I developed tricks to convince people I didn't have a weight problem. I'd wear black or dark tones with a jacket, which made me look skinny, of course. At group meals, I only ordered salads so people would think, "Oh look, she is doing her best to keep a good diet." After the meal, I'd hit a drive-through for my real food. Sometimes, I'd go to two different drive-throughs so the person working the window wouldn't judge the big woman ordering a meal that could feed two people. If I wanted cookies, I never bought one package. Instead, I'd buy two packages, a two-liter of Coke, and a gallon of ice cream. "Got a home full of boys tonight," I'd laugh at the cashier, who always gave me the courtesy of pretending to believe me.

Cosmetology departments were the worst. I'd circle the outside of the illuminated glass, afraid to walk down a center aisle and bust a thousand dollars' worth of perfumes. When I asked for a make-up or a lipstick sample, the saleswoman would always say, "You have very pretty eyes." In Shreveport, men had cat-called about everything except my eyes when I prissed down the assembly line. Now, men wouldn't bother to hold the door open for me. The only compliments were from saleswomen paid to tell me something nice. Even then, they could only compliment my eyes.

AT THE START OF 2008, the mayor of Oklahoma City, Mick Cornett, announced a new initiative for the entire city to lose weight. We were routinely ranked one of the country's unhealthiest cities and Mick had enough of hearing about it. It was the newest phase of the modern renaissance Oklahoma City had experienced over the last decade. After United Airlines had publicly rejected us in the early '90s, we decided to enact a little hope. We bet on ourselves to fix our own city and passed a new, one-cent sales tax for a program called MAPS. The central theme of the program was to tax ourselves to inject a bit of culture into our city. It started with building a new downtown baseball field and digging a canal through the abandoned warehouse district. The place would be called Bricktown. A lot of people laughed at the idea and said it was impossible. They said no one could turn abandoned warehouses into a teeming, family-friendly district of local tourism.

They were wrong.

With the MAPS program, evenings in Bricktown became electric delights. Restaurants opened and blues bands played along the canal filled with water taxis. A movie theater opened and even a sushi bar. The success of Bricktown and that first MAPS was the spark that ignited the fire of hope into other parts of the city. We passed two more MAPS tax plans over the next decade, launching new public parks downtown and an even bigger, newer arena. By 2008, there were whispers that Oklahoma City might get its own NBA team.

In other words, we enacted hope. After the United Airlines rejection, we took a painful, honest assessment of our city. We set a goal and wrote out the steps to accomplish that goal with MAPS. Then we summoned the courage, and our wallets, to pass the tax and start rebuilding our city from the inside out. After our first success in Bricktown, the hope of the entire city rose with the newly painted warehouses and massive arena. We started to believe nothing was impossible when a whole city acted in hope. So, it wasn't strange to hear our mayor's mission in 2008 for the city to go on a diet. He said we should all look less like elephants and more like ferrets. He set a goal for the city to lose one million collective pounds and put the program online for anyone to enroll. I was maybe the first of the forty-seven thousand to sign up.

FULL OF CONFIDENCE after enacting hope to get my degree, I was finally ready to tackle my weight problem. Like I said, hope isn't tame and will burn wildly into new areas of your life. I made my goal to lose

100 pounds in two years. That would leave me weighing 255 pounds, which to me sounded like I'd be a model for the Hanes *Just Her Size* campaign. My sister, Donna, had recently lost a lot of weight. Vicky lost seventy-five pounds on her Subway diet before the bombing. If they could do it, so could I. I took out my trusty ol' index cards and made a pretty short list: *Eat Salads for Lunch* and *Work Out 5 Days a Week.*

It took me two days to blow my schedule. By Friday, I was eating chocolate cake after my salad lunch. My years of routine shame and binging were too strong to beat in a week. But I didn't get down. Just like my journey in my education, I broke down my goals into smaller steps. This time laughing as I remembered Lynette's helpful phrase, "How do you eat an elephant?" My new list was simple. For the last two weeks of January, I would have no desserts and I'd do some walking on Saturdays and Sundays.

By the end of the month, I was eating donuts for breakfast and candy bar snacks in the afternoon because, you know, neither of those were technically desserts. I walked around my neighborhood a few times on the first Saturday. On Sunday, my legs were sore so I stayed in the house. The next Saturday, the day got away from me and I continued to avoid it all weekend.

In February, I doubled down with a meal plan from Jenny Craig. I told Lynette and everyone else at work about my walking plan so they'd keep me accountable.

Then I blew it again.

And again. And again.

And again. And again. And again.

By March, I decided an honest assessment of my weight was to accept it would never change. I was convinced my thyroid was the problem and modern science couldn't solve it. Other times, I was convinced my weight was so high my body chemistry couldn't drop it. I weighed too much to exercise to the intensity necessary to lose the weight. With all my talk of hope, it was hopeless. I'd finally found an impossible obstacle. I would carry the shame and the weight until I died. And, as my doctor explained at my last check up, death was a real concern. I was 41 years old with quickly-clogging arteries. Fatal heart disease for women my age at my size was common.

That spring, Lynette hired a business coach to spend some time with our executive team. Part of his coaching was to help us be better public speakers. I was still giving talks in a few small church groups and credit union functions, so I was glad to get some expert advice. The coach set up a video camera in our conference room and filmed us giving a five-minute speech. Later that month, we all sat in the conference room together as he went through each video, giving us tips on our hand gestures, timing, and voice tone. My video was last and the instant it finished I excused myself to the bathroom where I sobbed into the thin toilet paper for thirty minutes.

Watching my video in front of others felt like parading naked with my blue and black stretch marks on full display. I hadn't looked at a picture of myself for longer than five minutes for decades. It felt like torture to be stuck in that room, forced to witness the full gravity of my size. Those five minutes were too terrible for words and I couldn't handle it.

I tried to sneak back into my office after cleaning my face but Lynette caught me in the hall. "Have a seat," she pointed to her purple chairs. As soon as I sat down, she started, "I've had my stomach stapled." She went on to explain her own issues with body image and her weight. Pretty Lynette, who always seemed perfectly together, had a shameful secret. Or, at least, shameful for 2008. Stomach surgeries were still considered a form of cheating and often the shame of getting a surgery was more condemning than staying fat.

"I need a lot more than staples," I said, bouncing my arms off my bloated waist. "Besides, everyone will know if I do it."

"Amy," Lynette said gently, "if you have a destructive habit that is threatening your life, you must do everything possible to get rid of it. Even if you have to cut."

It sounded like the preacher's daughter coming out of her, echoing the scripture about cutting off your right hand if it caused you to sin. But those words struck me as one of the most solid laws of the universe. I remembered again how I'd begged my rescuers to cut off my leg so they could pull me free from the rubble. My shame was dealing a fatal blow to my spirit and my weight was absolutely threatening my life. I thought about Austin and how I wanted to be at his high school graduation. His college graduation. I wanted to dance at his wedding and rock a grandchild in my arms.

If my sheer willpower wasn't strong enough to rid my weight, then by God, I knew a surgeon's scalpel was sharp enough.

I WAS DEEP into my MBA program and used my newly acquired research skills to find every option available. I found a local organization called WeightWise that hosted free seminars and community engagement. The most common solution at the time for a woman my size was a gastric bypass. Essentially, the surgeons attached your intestines to the top of your stomach. The idea was to bypass the stomach almost altogether so there was literally no room to eat large meals. With the forced smaller meals, you'd lose weight. But the surgery was really risky and there were a lot of deaths from complications.

I knew the doctors at WeightWise were experts the moment I walked into the seminar. For starters, they knew their audience. The room had wide, comfortable chairs with strong cushions. During the presentations, they explained the options and reaffirmed my research. The best option without the grave danger of complications was something newer called a gastric sleeve. Rather than reroute your intestines, this procedure cut out three-fourths of your stomach. That resulted in the stomach taking on the shape of a tube or a "sleeve" which held much less food. So, just like the bypass, you would feel fuller sooner and, therefore, you'd eat less and lose weight.

"But you need to understand something," my surgeon said. "You'll lose a ton of weight for one year. But you'll gain it all back." He looked me dead in the eye, "And I mean *all* of it, unless you make a drastic change in your lifestyle. This only gives you a narrow window to save your life. Don't waste it."

They wouldn't schedule my surgery until I proved I was capable of changing my lifestyle. They demanded I lose ten percent of my body weight before they'd touch me. With all the balls rolling down the hill, I finally found the willpower and momentum to act. Besides, I'd lost ten percent of my body weight many times over my years of yo-yo diets. This time, though, I had the accountability of the WeightWise organization and a group of girls going through the same process with me. We chatted on message boards to encourage each other and shared tricks like buying egg drop soup and straining the egg shreds through a colander. I lost thirty-five pounds and my surgeons wheeled me into the operating room.

IN SOME WAYS, I failed at hope in my weight-loss journey. In other ways, hope was exactly what I accomplished. Sometimes, finding hope isn't about making smaller and smaller actions. Sometimes, there's no amount of courage or willpower that can reach the goal you've set. When that happens, your attempts at hope will fail, no matter how many times you try.

Maybe in a perfect world, we could all succeed at whatever step we can write. Whether it's engaging in the vulnerable talk with your spouse, or trying for the tenth time to get your child to care about school, or starting that fifth business start-up in your garage, or breaking your addiction to food, drugs, sex, tobacco, social media, or whatever else. But here in the real world, where we all live and breathe, we sometimes need to admit we don't have what it takes. We can't break the cycle. We don't have the courage.

But remember . . . there is *always* hope.

Sometimes you need to change your goal. Maybe instead of fixing your marriage, you need to redefine it. Maybe you need to take your child off your intellectual pedestal and figure out what they really care about. Maybe you should stop wasting time in business start-ups and team up with some other partners, sharing the profits together. If you're only five feet tall, maybe being a basketball star isn't a goal you can accomplish. But if you think about it, maybe being a star basketball player isn't your true desire. Maybe your real desire is to be great at any professional sport. So, go find something that fits a five-foot-tall athlete and train hard to succeed there.

In other words, there's always a path in hope. You may need to consider your goal and redefine it so it describes what you actually care about. For me, I had to redefine my goal from *Losing 100 Pounds by Myself* to *Losing 100 Pounds by Any Means Possible*. In a way, my goal didn't actually change. I could still lose weight. I just needed to redefine the destination. I needed to be honest that, for whatever reason, I couldn't lose that much weight on my own. But with a surgeon's help, hope made it possible.

OKLAHOMA CITY STOLE an NBA team from Seattle. At least, that's what Seattle claimed. A group of Oklahoma City business leaders bought the team from Howard Shultz, the founder of Starbucks, stating they had no intention of moving the team out of Seattle. After some pretty complicated problems arose concerning Seattle's arena, the new Oklahoma City-based owners moved the team to Oklahoma City. Of course, everyone with half a brain knew they would try it the moment they announced their negotiations with Mr. Shultz. Everyone involved knew about the new arena we'd built with MAPS and how desperate we wanted a professional sports team. In the end, after a lawsuit and a very public settlement of millions of dollars, the team was allowed to move.

We called the new team the Oklahoma City Thunder and our new arena was sold out every game in their first season, which turned out to be one of the worst seasons of any basketball team in history. The Thunder were rock bottom of the league, averaging two lost games for every win. It seemed like the entire nation sneered at us, laughing at our just rewards for our perceived theft. The common shared line was, "Did we really expect anything different from a place like Oklahoma City?"

MY WEIGHT TOOK an aggressive drop a month after my surgery. Over the next seven months, I lost one hundred pounds. My coworkers kept asking what I'd done. Was it the walking? Jenny Craig? Asparagus? Rice cakes? I had a choice. Only Lynette knew I'd done the surgery. And, like Lynette, I could keep it a secret. Image means a lot for executives and I knew they'd judge me for taking the easy way out. They'd say, of course, big Amy's only shot at losing weight was cheating. They'd call me weak and forever label me as a woman with no real strength of her own.

But I was done with shame ruling my life. I never wanted another moment of sheer terror like when I'd felt exposed watching my true self move on the TV in the conference room. I would never again allow my true self to haunt my mind. If I was going to shed my weight, I'd be darn sure to shed all my shame with it.

"I got a gastric sleeve surgery," I answered loudly whenever I was asked, my unburdened back as straight as a longleaf pine.

2017 Ironman Arizona

Hour Twelve

I CHEATED. Well, not really. I didn't cut the course or use steroids. I cheated on my personal fuel plan. You see, besides making the time cuts, the most important part of a triathlon is your nutrition plan, which we call our fuel. The body can't store enough energy to propel through an Ironman. The body also can't break fat down into energy fast enough to finish. A triathlete will burn somewhere between 7,000 and 10,000 calories on race day. Considering the body can only store up to 2,000 calories of ready-to-burn carbohydrates, you've got to bridge over 5,000 calories throughout the race.

Then there's the issue of hydration, which is a lot more complicated than drinking water. During a heavy activity like an Ironman, athletes can lose one liter of sweat every hour. Those 32 ounces are highly concentrated with body salt. So, with the calories you need to ingest, you need to also to replenish your salt and water along the way. It gets even more complex from there. Everyone's burn rate of calories is different. Every body breaks fat down into energy at a different rate. The amount of salt in our sweat and the volume of sweat lost per hour varies dramatically, too. Then there's the environment to consider. In hot temperatures, you burn more energy trying to stay cool and lose more sweat. Then on top of all that is your digestive tract's sensitivities in processing gluten, nuts, dairy, processed sugar, soy, and everything else.

So, a big part of triathlon training is figuring out the right fuel plan for your individual body. Consume too much extra salt and you'll dehydrate yourself, forcing all the water out of your muscles. Consume too little salt and you'll be dehydrated by not retaining enough water in your muscles. Eat too much fat and you'll waste energy digesting food that can't be used for energy for another few hours. Eat too many carbs and you'll feel the sugar crash an hour later, completely exhausting your efforts. Eat something your digestive tract is even slightly sensitive to and you'll be racing to every port-a-potty on the course.

When you screw up your fuel, you bonk. I'm pretty sure that's the official medical term, too. Bonking throws you into a haze and your body stops responding. It can be so dangerous for the high-performance athletes that permanent brain damage can occur. Lance Armstrong once bonked on a leg of the Tour de France and admitted he could have lost his ability to bike forever if it wasn't for a competitor pulling in close to let Lance draft the final miles of the race.

I bonked at mile three in the run. I don't know how or when, but my fuel was wrong and it caught up to me. My body is the kind that can't consume too many simple sugars. I'm fine digesting them, but the crash I feel an hour later is so devasting that it keeps me from finishing long workouts. So instead of Gatorade with all its sugar, I have a tube of base salt in my jersey, which is basically a portable salt lick. I pop the cap, lick my thumb, cover the tube with my thumb, shake the tube, and then lick my salt-crusted thumb. Then I quickly gulp water to relieve the stinging sensation on my tongue. The only carbohydrates I found that I could consume while sustaining my performance were my Uncrustables. The protein kept my insulin spike at a minimum so I wouldn't crash an hour later.

I didn't know if it was the hydration or the calories that caused my bonk. I only knew I could barely walk and there were twenty-three miles farther to run. I tried to calm my mind and tell myself it would pass. My body just needed a little more time to break down some fat into energy. I took a couple licks of salt, just in case it was hydration. Then I freaked out, wondering if I'd been taking in too much salt, so I drank a bunch of water at the next water stop.

Nothing changed. I refused to walk because it felt like once I started, I'd never make it to the finish line. So, I kept my arms pumping and imagined my feet kicking higher behind me with every stride. Then a couple of women passed me in a brisk walk. It deflated my effort and I stopped to stretch my legs. I overheard the women talking about the next time cut-off. I had forgotten there was a cut-off in the middle of the run at ten o'clock. I only had a couple of hours to make it and, at the pace I was moving, I'd never make it. I didn't have time for my bonk to pass. If something didn't change soon, the officials would remove my ankle band and brand me forever with the DNF.

So, I cheated on my fuel plan. At the next water stop, I snatched a can of Coke. Real Coke, with all its sugary goodness. It was way too early in my run and I knew I'd have the sugar crash of all sugar crashes hit me in an hour. But if I didn't do something now, I wouldn't last another hour. At the next station, I ate a handful of pretzels, a banana, and had a few sips of Red Bull.

Then I charged down the course.

Chapter Eight

Climbing

EIGHT MONTHS after my gastric sleeve surgery, I stood on the scale in my bathroom and felt the blood drain from my face. It was the end of December and I'd just finished the final gauntlet of holiday feasts. To my horror, my weight loss had reversed and I'd gained three pounds. Instead of losing 100 pounds since my surgery, now I'd only lost 97. My surgeon's warning whispered like a ghost in the shower's steam. The surgery was never meant to be permanent. It would only give me a window of time to change my lifestyle.

And now that window was closing.

For the past eight months, I'd spent my mornings in the bathroom swinging my arms in glee. It's a strange sensation to lose 100 pounds. I passed my hand through space my body used to fill. I expected my hand to contact my hip or my belly, but now it didn't. I'd look down and expect to see my chest sticking out from my chin, but now I saw the ground. It would make me twitch and I'd have to catch myself from a sensation of vertigo, like I'd just leaned against a wall that decided to move an inch.

The familiar bulges evaporated into loose creases. My stomach touched itself in new places when I sat or, to my excitement, when I bent over. Because, yes, I could finally bend over. The sensations of new, fresh skin-to-skin contact were a little exotic, the way it used to feel when I was younger and a fancy bra would tug under my arm. Of course, I still couldn't buy fancy lingerie. I couldn't even look at myself in the mirror without clothes. The weight dissipated but my skin hadn't. Instead of rolls of fat tumbling over my thighs, I had sagging drapes like an old elephant. Thin, coiled white wrinkles wriggled up, down, crossways, and other ways on my empty pockets of skin. The old blue and black stretch marks still scarred my body. And the best way to describe my breasts would be to call them rocks in socks. Large, wrinkled, striped socks. Lucky for me, I was really good at dissociating from my body. It was intriguing in a freaky way, but still a foreign object in my mind. I had to wait until I was clothed before recognizing myself, after I'd layered and tucked my folds carefully into my Spanx and blouses, keeping my belt fastened tight so an Oklahoma gust wouldn't billow my loose skin and blow me into the sky like a renegade kite.

I cried that December morning. Over the last month, I'd reignited the pilot light of my insatiable hunger. The gastric sleeve was working as intended to keep me from eating a lot of food at one time, but I discovered a work around. I could literally eat a gallon of kettle corn in a single sitting because the instantly dissolving kernels of butter and sugar didn't overstuff my new gastric sleeve stomach. I'd lost the weight, but I hadn't changed my lifestyle. I was on the path back to being large. Only this time, I would be truly hopeless. There's no such thing as a *second* gastric sleeve surgery.

I called the closest gym to my house. Well, the closest local gym without the intimidating bicep-bulging advertisements and gold-skinned women in bikinis. "I know it's not for fat people," I said on the phone to the gym's owner. It was the third time I'd talked to him in two days. "I'll just lose a little more weight at home so I won't break your treadmill."

"No, Amy," the owner sighed. "the gym is made *for* bigger people.

That's the whole point." I didn't believe him. Exercise was a bizarre mystery to me. I had never intentionally exercised in my forty-two years of life. Telling someone I would exercise was like telling someone I'd run a marathon. Or walk on the moon. Exercise was something other people did, over *there*.

I finally mustered the courage to walk into Cross Trainers at 6 a.m. at the end of January. I had been wrong. Exercise wasn't like walking on the moon. It was like walking onto a spaceship. Bright white lights blared from every direction. A guy with strange chunks of muscles coiling and uncoiling on his back yanked thick black ropes attached to the wall. A couple of girls bounced on treadmills so quickly their bleached pony tails seemed to be in zero gravity, wafting in slow motion. A few others looked like Sigourney Weaver in *Aliens*, sweating inside exoskeleton machines with an excessive number of levers.

I saw my reflection in at least five different mirrors across the gym's walls and knew everyone else saw the same five versions of the odd duck wobbling into the gym. I got onto an elliptical but couldn't figure out the buttons, so I walked on a treadmill for a few minutes. I kept my head focused on the red lights on the screen, trying not to look at my jiggling fat in the mirror on my left or the girl on my right blowing bubble gum as she walked up a revolving staircase. After five minutes, I couldn't take another step and I limped out of the gym, embarrassed under the bright lights and stares of real athletes.

My weight crept up another five pounds. Soon, I'd only lost 93 pounds since my surgery. My friends at work convinced me to try some other exercises with the same fizzled results. Pilates and yoga didn't work for me. The mats were too narrow and even though I could bend over now, my extra skin kept me from doing a full forward fold. I eventually tried some of the weight machines, but it took me so long to adjust the seats and levers my back started to ache before I'd finished my first set. And don't get me started on Zumba. A friend and I did one class and the instructor politely asked that I never come back. Our giggles had echoed on the wooden floors louder than the music.

I tried to explain we'd been laughing at the sound of the loud clap my flaps of belly skin made whenever I tried a goofy pelvic thrust, but I didn't try too hard. Besides, how could we *not* laugh in a room full of grown women slapping their own butts?

"Come bike with me," Lynette said one day.

"Oh, no," I said. "You aren't getting me in those diaper pants." It was the name I gave the pants my sister wore when she rode. Donna had been biking for years now. She'd drunk the Kool-Aid of the cycling groups, which required you to wear bright helmets on uncomfortable bikes with special shoes that clipped into the pedals. The funniest garment in her get-up was the pair of spandex pants with a thick cushion down the backside. I'm sure the cushion helped with the coaster-thin seats, but it looked like an adult diaper.

"Not like that," Lynette insisted. She showed me pictures of cruiser bikes she'd bought with her husband. They looked normal, like the bikes I rode as a kid. The seat was low. The handlebars high. And the pedals didn't require clipping in. "It will be fun," she said.

"Are you sure it will handle my weight?" I asked. I still weighed close to 270 pounds. Lynette shot me a look and pointed at the thick tires. They weren't like the thin discs Donna rode on. I agreed, but mostly because my scale that morning showed some new pounds. I had to figure something out soon.

A few days later, we met at Lynette's house off the shore of Lake Overholser after work. I wore jeans with a drawstring waist, tennis shoes, and a windbreaker (although I don't think they call them windbreakers anymore). I was relieved to see Lynette wearing something similar, with sweats and a jacket.

"Here." Lynette handed me a helmet with a thick foam rim and splashes of neon green across the top.

"I'm going to look silly," I said, unsure of the point. I wouldn't be breaking any speed records today. Lynette ignored me and strapped on an even brighter helmet.

"I'm not sure I remember how," I said.

"You'll be fine," Lynette said, leaning off the ground and starting down the paved trail next to the shore. "It's just like riding a bike."

I was out of chances to stall. Lynette was quickly getting away from me, heading toward the orange sky of the setting sun. I eased over the seat and tested my weight. The bike didn't groan. The tires stayed inflated. I put an uncertain foot on a pedal and tested a small push.

The fresh air rushed into my face. The pavement streaked beneath my feet. In three breaths, I moved my body faster and further than I'd traveled in twenty years. My lungs swelled with the sweet lake air, a mix of dandelions and rock-rich water.

And it was so easy. So . . . exhilarating. A long-forgotten door inside me was suddenly kicked out to reveal the world. Wild earth swept through the stale rooms of my soul. How had I forgotten about the world? I giggled. A few tears streamed past my temples. A bug flew into my grinning teeth. I kept pedaling and basked in the nature gushing all around me.

We finished in fifteen minutes. That's all it took to be reborn.

"Thank you for letting me do that," I said with a forced level tone. Lynette smiled and I wobbled on jelly legs to my car.

As soon as I plopped inside, I called Donna. "I want a bike."

The next weekend Donna took me to Pro Bike. I bought a cruiser bike like Lynette's, even though Donna argued I should buy the complicated road bike with special shoe clips and the tiny seat you could only ride in diaper pants. "I'm not crazy like you guys," I said as I paid.

"Sure," the bike shop owner smiled.

Donna and I rode around Lake Hefner. I expected the ride to be less dramatic than my first, the way a movie hits you softer on your second viewing, but it was even more powerful. We went the full ten miles around the lake. Ten miles! I'd never fathomed I could push my body that far in a year.

"How'd you like it?" Donna asked.

"It's, uh," I stumbled, "you won't understand."

"Yes, I do."

"I mean, even I don't understand. It's like, like—"

"It's like riding horses in Shreveport." She nailed it. It was like riding Freddy in the woods with my dad. It was like longleaf pines breaking away to a crystalline lake. It was the smell of wet leaves and a choir of songbirds. It was sunburns and whistling wind. It was a boundless blue sky and a horizon that beckoned my soul.

"I can't believe I've waited all this . . . oh, God!" I screamed. A searing pain sliced up my thigh as I dismounted. I thought I'd pulled something in my thigh. I'd be bedridden for weeks and the weight would pile back. I'd be large again with no hope. The fat would clog my arteries and I'd die.

But, no, it wasn't a torn muscle. It was my skin. I'd worn my jeans again and the inseam had rubbed me raw. "Don't even say it," I told Donna. "I'll just wear sweats next time."

"Sure," she smiled.

By the end of the summer, I bought a road bike. The owner at Pro Bike even held my seat as I learned to balance on the thin disc tires. I asked for a deal since this was my second bike to buy from him. He smiled and offered me a pair of diaper pants, no charge.

WE CHANGED the name of FECU to Allegiance Credit Union. The name Federal Employees Credit Union didn't match our membership base anymore. After our years of successful transformation under Lynette's leadership, federal employees made up a small number of our growing accounts. The name didn't fit our market. We considered shortening our official name to just the letters FECU, but someone figured out that merging those letters into a single word could sound like a curse word.

In some ways, changing our name shed the last remnants of the pre-bombing credit union, but in other ways the name change preserved it. We keep a small garden with two fountains at our headquarters. The larger fountain's water flows over chunks of the imploded building granite inscribed with the names of those who died.

Sonja's name is written there with Vicky and everyone else who deserved to live. The second fountain is a little smaller and off to the side. It jets straight up from the ground like an ever-changing flower of water. We call it our Fountain of Hope. As long as the Fountain of Hope springs from the ground, the lasting memories of my fallen friends live on.

OVER THE NEXT YEARS, I became a total cyclepath. Ever since I moved to Oklahoma City, I'd confined myself inside a building or a car, traveling the same twelve miles between home and work. When it rained, it splashed the glass. When the seasons changed, I turned the dial on my dash or thermostat. I remained dry and comfortable in the recycled air of offices, cars, restaurants, and houses. Cycling shattered my comfort and I was exposed again.

Donna and I charted a foodie ride through forty-five miles of the city on Saturday mornings. We'd meet near my house and have a donut before riding around Lake Overholser. Then we'd cycle through the city streets to Lake Hefner, where we'd grab a fresh kolache. Then we'd head through the city streets again to Big Truck Tacos for a breakfast burrito. It may sound like a pleasant ride, but it was hardly that. Pleasant is what you call a painting or a well-mannered waiter. We cycled on the sharp edge of danger. A popped tire could send you reeling headfirst into the pavement. A driver's quick turn could crush you, even if you're wearing a bright pink helmet, a bright pink jacket, and riding a bright pink bike. I'll never understand it, but there's a very ugly aggression in some drivers, young and old, against cyclists. "Fat ass!" a kid yelled one afternoon with his head so far out the window I felt his spit on my cheek. I've had a McDonald's cup of orange Hi-C hit my back, plastic Coke bottles, and once a half-full bag of Skittles.

But those people don't bother me as much as the drivers who try to kill me. Drivers never appreciate how far their side-view mirrors stick out, or how the wind stream of their car can suck a cyclist under their tires. I have to ride with a quarter-sized mirror attached to my helmet to keep a hawk eye on the vehicles approaching, often pulling muscles in my neck in a sudden jerk to avoid the wind stream sucking me into the car. Almost every year, a cyclist I've met dies because a driver couldn't be bothered to skootch their steering wheel over an inch.

The adventure brought me joy. The normal, everyday deadlines and personnel problems at work stopped bothering me. A bad number on an expense report or petty squabble over approval authority was nothing compared to a car trying to kill me. The thrill of my rides made work a smaller part of my life. I made friends outside the office. I had stories to share full of suspense and danger. I finally had a life outside of work.

MY FIRST TRIP around Lake Hefner had been ten miles. At the time, that was like saying I'd gone a hundred miles. They were both the same level of impossible. And yet, I'd done the impossible. Over the next years, I kept pushing the numbers to see where my limit was. I cycled twice around Lake Hefner. Our Saturday morning foodie rides were forty-five miles round trip. I joined some local group rides, soon going as far as seventy miles on a single day. And I kept pushing my limit.

I learned about an event called Oklahoma Freewheel. In the middle of summer, a group of cyclists traveled for seven days through the back roads of Oklahoma in 90-degree temperatures, sleeping in tents along the way. In other words, it was insane and I signed myself up. Then I signed Donna up. Less than one year after getting my road bike, I'd cover 500 miles in seven days. It sounded impossible. But in a way, I was an impossible addict. There was an intoxicating feeling when I tried something impossible, hearing everyone tell me it was crazy, and then doing it anyway. I fell in love with beating the unbeatable odds.

It was kind of like trying on new dresses at the department store. Before my surgery, I'd only been able to buy clothes at Catherine's. Now, even though my skin kept me deep in the double-digit sizes, I took a trip to the mall every weekend. I spent hours in the dressing room trying on armloads of blouses and pants. Some stores had to give me two signs to add together for the number of items I hauled into the changing room. I'd gone from only one option to something close to a million and I wanted to discover the new boundaries of my body. I needed to understand where I fit, and where I didn't.

I used my vacation for the week-long Freewheel in June 2010. That year, the organizers took us to the eastern side of Oklahoma, pushing from the Texas border up to Kansas. For seven days we slept in hot tents, woke early, and spent five hours cycling up hills in the oppressive heat. The early mornings were spiritual with cricket symphonies in wild grass, the sun's golden sheen on wheat fields, and single-stop-sign towns with the best pancakes with real maple syrup. I'd gotten into the habit of praying during the first miles of the day. I'd thank God for the health of my legs, the fresh breath in my lungs, and being alive to experience our earth. But by the last hours of our rides, I would curse every hill He'd created and commit all forms of blasphemy, begging the Nordic gods of the frozen sea for a single cloud to block the sun.

In the middle of the week, we took on the Staircase Mountains. Have you ever tried to pedal a bike up a staircase? Of course not. Only a crazy person would try. The mountain range was probably more like foothills compared to the Rockies, but looking up from the bottom it looked like Everest. A flock of birds flew above us, at the same level as the rising, twisting road. If I had a limit, surely this was it.

"Are you ready?" Donna asked. I knew what she meant. She was saying *I don't think you're ready.* And she was right. I wasn't. She'd been cycling for five years. I'd been on a road bike for one. I'd bought my first clip-ins pedals only a few weeks ago. The clip-ins helped me pull up on the pedal with one leg as I pushed down with the other, which gave more power with every rotation, something essential for cycling up a mountain. But I didn't have my pulling muscles developed yet. It was around that time I realized I wasn't a cyclepath. I was just stupid. Plain and simple.

"I'll give it the ol' college try," I said as I pushed down. I knew it was impossible. I knew I couldn't make it. I had my tennis shoes in my bag and soon I'd be walking my bike up the mountain.

But somehow, I did it. Somehow, Donna and I rode into camp before the end of the afternoon. I can't explain how. I just kept pedaling. When it got hard, when my muscles burned, I kept pedaling. It was slow. It was agonizing. But I pedaled through the pain and made it. In fourteen months, I'd gone from getting jelly legs after a fifteen-minute pleasure ride to powering my body twenty miles up a mountain. Even to my own ears, it sounded like a miracle. I thought maybe I had a secret power. Maybe I was some kind of wonder woman.

"I bet I could do a century ride," I told our friends on the road the next morning. A century ride to cyclists is essentially what a marathon is for runners. It's the gold standard, the pinnacle challenge separating true cyclists from amateurs. It's one hundred miles in a single day. I'd heard the other cyclists talk about century rides in our group training and especially during the long hours of the Freewheel. They wore their t-shirts from century rides in New Orleans and Texas with pride.

"You sure can," an old man with a goatee agreed near me.

"Thank you," I said, encouraged.

"Of course," the man snarled, "anyone can, given enough time."

I laughed and moved on, but he was right. Every time a century ride was mentioned, someone dropped a detail of how fast they'd done it. I'd missed the time component because I thought riding one hundred miles in a single day was the achievement. I started to second-guess everything I'd accomplished so far. I'd been so focused on the *number* of miles, I hadn't thought about my time. Donna and I had conquered Staircase Mountain, sure, but we'd been the last ones to coast down the other side. I wasn't a wonder woman after all.

I trained harder after the Freewheel. In the winter months, I went back to the spaceship gym to ride the indoor bikes, this time not caring about my jiggling arms as I powered up the resistance. On group rides, I climbed up from the slow pace to the medium pace group. In six months, I advanced from an average of twelve miles per hour to sixteen. But that wasn't enough. My addiction to the impossible needed something real and tangible. A true test. I wanted a story the old man couldn't discount.

So I signed up for a ride in Wichita Falls called the Hotter'N Hell Hundred.

IN A SINGLE YEAR, something wild happened to the Oklahoma City Thunder. We started winning. A lot. We had three all-star caliber players in Kevin Durant, Russell Westbrook, and James Harden. Seemingly overnight, we transformed from a team of confused rookies to a dynamic trio of aggressive threats. One year after our terrible season, we made it to the playoffs. The next year we went deep into the playoffs. And the year after that, we made it to the NBA Finals. Everybody started to say something different about us. They scratched their heads and asked, "Who could have guessed this from a place like Oklahoma City?"

The change was bigger than sports. Across the city, microbreweries appeared next to remodeled theatres. A giant new glass tower was built. Smaller districts of entertainment and culture peppered outside of downtown. The Thunder's exciting games matched the city's spirit. The power of the MAPS programs had injected a vibrant culture into our city.

For years, when we'd traveled and mentioned we were from Oklahoma City, people tilted their heads and mentioned the bombing. The children and the dead. McVeigh and the death penalty. Sadness. Lost innocence. Evil. But after the Thunder, those comments stopped. Now, wherever I traveled, people would say something about Durant or Westbrook. They talked about unbelievable victory. That was our city's new brand. No one thought about the Penn Square Bank crash. No one remembered United Airlines rejecting our astronomical offer. Our city had transformed from the inside out and had become an example to the world of the awesome power of authentic hope.

THE HOTTER'N HELL HUNDRED (or as we cyclepaths call it, the Triple-H) was one hundred miles in the burning August sun in Texas, often reaching one hundred degrees. It was timed and had a cut-off at a place called Hell's Gate. If you didn't make it past the gate before noon, they sent you on an easier and shorter route to finish the day. In other words, it was so hot they refused to let you risk serious bonking or worse by staying on the course for too long.

I had some serious training to do if I was going to make it through Hell's Gate in time. So I took out my index cards and came up with a list. I'll spare you some of my screw-ups this time and just give you the answer I landed on. If I could cycle to work, I could get enough miles in a week to keep increasing my speed. That sounds nice, but I couldn't be a vice president wearing my cycling clothes and drenched in sweat every day. I thought about that new problem for a few weeks until I remembered we had an unused and unfinished locker room next to the bathrooms with some unfinished plumbing. I talked to Lynette about it and she agreed to let me take freezing cold showers from the spigot with no head every morning. She even let me drape my sweaty bike spandex on the ledge of her balcony to dry. I spent that spring and all through the hot summer riding to work and showering at the office before anyone else was there. Then I rode my bike back home around four, narrowly missing the worst of the five o'clock traffic.

Training for the Triple-H gave me a quantum leap in my leadership. I'd gotten my MBA and I'd been the Vice President of Operations for ten years now. I'd been working at Allegiance for over twenty. Whenever a problem surfaced, I had a strategy in mind in minutes. It was easy when you had that kind of history in the same company. I'd been there through every change. From before dial-up internet to wi-fi. From print newspapers to blogs. Desk calculators to Excel. Pagers to iPhones. I knew every system and process inside and out because I'd helped create most of them. For almost every position, I knew the two people who had held the position before and what worked best for each of their personalities. Whatever the issue, I knew exactly who to talk to and when to start the path toward a solution.

My philosophy on coaching others had always been the same: work hard to see the problem and work hard to fix the problem. I invested the majority of my days leading others to become better at work. I spent my energy drawing out their natural talents and encouraging them to use those talents in the next work project. This wasn't something they taught in my MBA program. You can't learn it from a book. It was something I learned through the examples of Vicky and Lynette. I spent all my efforts encouraging others to be their best at work. I wanted everyone to share in the fulfillment I'd discovered by grinding the days and weeks in the office and feeling the joy when your work paid off.

But cycling revealed the huge blind spot in my leadership philosophy. I'd fallen for the lie that work was life. To me, joy was only found by being amazing at your job. That was the fulfillment Vicky had shown me in my early years. It was the example Lynette had shown me, which had driven me into the classroom. I had kept and used all my energy focused on work success, thinking there was no other place to find a sense of empowerment or self-fulfillment. When cycling reawakened the withered limbs of my soul, I realized I'd been doing it wrong. There was so much joy outside the four walls of the office. Risking adventure outdoors had made my office problems small, which was the size office problems should have always been. And now I wanted to share this revelation with everyone.

I started inviting my employees to cycle to work with me. I advertised my cycling life in the pictures in my office, my postings on social media, and in my loudest voice in the hallways. I wanted everyone to discover what I had: the path to fulfilling yourself was right outside the office windows. I encouraged others to talk about what they did at home. Fishing, music, art, or whatever. I'd bring up their non-work lives at the start of department-head meetings and we'd trade stories of impassioned side projects or sports like college football and, of course, the Oklahoma City Thunder.

Finding joy in cycling made me see my colleagues in a fresh light. I saw them as more than colleagues. I saw them as individuals with passions and love outside the office. I began to create newer, more authentic relationships with people I'd known for years. I invested in their whole person, including their lives at home.

These days, there is a ton of research, data, and trainings on the exponential improvement to productivity when leadership focuses on encouraging life outside the office. At the time, I'd never read those journals. Maybe it's bad to say (so please don't tell my board), but I didn't make this philosophy change to improve the numbers at work. All I wanted to do was share my joy.

I still believe joy starts by working to master your craft at work. I know firsthand that being bad at your job sucks, even if you can hide it from yourself or others. It makes you feel bad about yourself and you project your low esteem onto everyone around you. So, of course, you should first be good at your job. But then remember total fulfillment is outside your job. And even though it sounds contradictory, reaching your fulfillment outside your job will actually increase your productivity and energy in your job. But then again, maybe that shouldn't sound contradictory. If you want to reach your human potential, be a total human.

Looking back now, I think that was why Lynette gave me permission to shower at work and stretch out my bike clothes like a banner on her balcony. She could have easily declined my requests. She could have politely asked me to keep my volume down. *It's great to bike, dear, but leave home life at home.* But I think she'd seen how much more productive I could become by finally finding joy outside the office. She knew once I learned the credit union supported all of me, cycling and all, that I'd become even more devoted to our work. Lynette had helped me get my education and lose my weight. She'd introduced me to cycling. And now, here she was again, still lifting me into higher altitudes of leadership.

OKLAHOMA IS a humid place. While cycling in Oklahoma Freewheel, the warm moisture in the air was so thick we'd joke that you could smell the heat. I thought that would make my ride at Triple-H easier than others who weren't from humid climates. But all my confidence evaporated when I stepped into the Texas sun on the Friday before the race. The heat stung me. Like, it actually hurt my skin and I swore I could hear my sweat sizzling on my skin. In the fifty steps from my car to the hotel lobby, beads of sweat rolled down my back and under my armpits. *I'm not going to make it*, I thought. Even though Staircase Mountain had seemed impossible a year before, this was unfathomable. Only professionals could make it one hundred miles in this heat.

By the time I'd gotten into my hotel room and blasted the window air conditioning unit, I'd abandoned the goal on my note card saying *Pass Hell's Gate*. Instead, I would be fine with taking the shorter, re-routed course of only seventy-five miles to the finish. In this heat, I wasn't sure if I'd even manage that far. I imagined striking through my previous goal and writing down two new goals: *Don't Pass Out* and *Don't Die*.

Flames spewed from the canon that fired at the start line. There were eleven thousand cyclists packed butt cheek to butt cheek in the street. It was five minutes before I could stop skateboarding down the street with shuffling feet and clip into my pedals. I gulped all of my water bottle one mile from the start because it felt like I'd already shed eight ounces of sweat.

"His mercies are new every morning," I said out loud to the rising sun as we scootched along.

"Is that the Bible or something?" a woman in front of me turned her head to ask. She didn't seem to like the Bible.

"Yeah," I said, adding quickly, "It's just something I say every race."

"Hey, I'll take all the mercy I can get today." She turned back and maneuvered her bike through the crowded cyclists. The back of her shirt had upside down lettering reading, *BUT IS MY BIKE OKAY?*

The excitement was high until the mass of cyclists thinned out after the first ten miles. The gaps between cyclists grew larger and larger. That's when the pain started. It always begins in my hamstrings. It's a tightness that indicates I'm in the good zone, a solid pace in a slightly uncomfortable distance. On the Freewheel, I never leave this stage. I keep myself in that zone, my bones staying warm. But I was at Triple-H and time was of the essence. I couldn't stay comfortable. As the cyclist ahead of me pulled away, I shifted into a new gear to catch up.

Then the tightness gripped my quads and calves. I felt discomfort everywhere. My mind suggested I should stop moving so fast, the way you might consider rolling over when you've been laying wrong on the living room floor. It was a polite request, but stern. *Please, stop. This isn't good.* It was a creaking, growing pain that yearned for relief. This is where I stayed during my training to create tiny tears in all my muscles. After an hour or so, I'd stop and congratulate myself. I'd be sore for a few days and all the stronger next week. But, again, I was at Triple-H and I couldn't stop after an hour. I had to keep at it for eighty more miles. So, I kept pedaling.

The tightness flickered in my chest and it started to feel difficult to fill my lungs with enough oxygen. I imagined each breath was cooling the heat in my thighs. But it got hotter. The next change didn't take long. It was like a backdraft in an apartment fire. In one moment, I had the fire at bay. In the next moment, my entire body was engulfed with a white fire of pain.

And I loved it.

This is my dirty little secret of cycling. Maybe the bombing broke something in my brain, but then again there were eleven thousand cyclists at the race that shared my same paradox. I don't bike to keep the weight off, although that's pretty awesome. I don't bike to risk danger, but it does reduce my stress. I don't bike for the races, even though I like wearing medals.

I bike to burn.

IT'S A DIFFICULT CONCEPT to explain because, at its core, it doesn't make sense. It's a bit irrational to say I don't like pain but I seek it. The best way to explain the sensation is to describe three fires that rage in my moments of intense endurance. I don't actually think of it in three fires, but it's the only way I can write down the abstract, unexplainable experience.

The first fire I've already described. It's the searing iron in your quads, hamstrings, and calves. It's the flame of physical pain.

The second fire comes a little time after. It's the inferno in your mind. The world around you is burned away. Your past memories are cinders. Your future goals are smoke. All that exists is the instantly vanishing and reappearing present. This moment is a torrent of fire swirling behind your eyes, like a hurricane in hell. It swelters in a mighty wind declaring, "You can't do this." It's not a challenge. It's a fact. It's a law of nature. An uncontested, universal truth. You cannot pedal one more rotation. To try is suicide.

Then there's the third fire. It's the smallest of the three. To me, it's a thin pink flame that whispers into the storm, "Watch me." It reaches in front of me and slices through the inferno, splitting the funnel of fire. It's a flicker of my soul. It's the fire of hope.

I feel closest to my spirit when the three fires wage their war. The sensation is like the climax of a good underdog movie. If the movie is good, it's convinced you for a moment the underdog can't do it. Rocky has fallen and can't get up. War Admiral passes Seabiscuit. You've watched the movie for two hours to feel this moment, these thirty seconds, suddenly tricked into believing the bad guy will win. But then he doesn't. Rocky knocks him out. Seabiscuit's legs finds a new cadence and he wins by five strides. The three fires are like these moments, except it lasts for thirty *minutes*. Time seems to evaporate and there is only the knowledge that I can't possibly push another pedal, and yet I do.

CYCLISTS AT TRIPLE-H don't bike one hundred miles without

stopping. Like most events, there are a number of water stops and medical tents set up along the way, many with interesting themes. There were country bands and DJs. Girls in grass skirts serving shots of pickle juice slushies and Halloween-costumed witches with big pumpkin bowls of extra-salted Fritos. I stopped at every single one. I gulped the water, downed the pickle shots, and poured the coldest liquid I could find down my neck and the back of my legs. The hazy mirage of glass down the distant road was so strong it seemed to pierce my sunglasses and blind my eyes.

"It's officially the hottest temperature ever recorded," said a girl with a coconut bra and violent sunburns on her bare shoulders.

"There's another SAG wagon," someone mentioned. A truck rolled slowly down the street with a trailer hauling a pile of twisted bike frames and tires. Cyclists sat in the back, staring down into the black asphalt with swollen and red-veined eyes. They were the cyclists who had quit the race because of a busted bike or heat exhaustion. I darted my gaze somewhere else, afraid of making eye contact. I was afraid I'd feel their shame and break into tears.

My miles per hour dropped between every stop. I lagged longer. The heat rose and rose. Twenty miles from Hell's Gate, I knew it was over for me. Even if I kept my current speed for the next twenty miles, I'd miss the cut-off. I envisioned my index card again and the new goal I'd made yesterday: *Don't Pass Out.*

"They're closing Hell's Gate early," a volunteer said.

"It hit 109 degrees already," someone else mentioned.

"It's even hotter on the asphalt."

"I saw a guy with his tire melted."

"Bull."

"No joke. I saw it. Little squiggling lines all down the tread."

"I heard they called in three extra SAG wagons."

"Well, there's no way I'll make it this year."

On and on the conversation trailed. There was no motion in it. No one sounded worried. It was the hottest temperature the event had ever recorded. I checked my watch. Even if Hell's Gate wasn't closed early, no one at this stop would make it.

I was surprised that it felt good. I was soggy from sweat. The humidity seemed to steam in my lungs. I poured water three times into the same full water bottle because I couldn't think straight. Here I was, twenty miles from Hell's Gate, and I'd found my limit. There was no shame in it. The guys around me didn't seem to mind. Some of them smiled. I'd only been on my road bike for two years and I'd pushed just as hard as the veterans around me. I'd taken Staircase Mountain. I'd completed two Freewheels. Completing the shorter, 75-mile course in the hottest temperatures ever recorded in Triple-H's history was an accomplishment. A proud one. I'd tested myself and finally found where I fit. At least I would survive the day.

Then again, I thought, *What the hell?*

I clipped in and pushed, leaving the boys behind. I imagined my legs were cannons, spewing flames with every rotation. I dropped into the three fires again and again. I bit my cheek when the pain gripped my legs. I didn't look at my watch. I barely registered the road. I passed a water stop. I was the torrent and the torrent was me. I swirled around the world and the universe swirled inside me. My pink flame of hope kept its focus and cleaved through the inferno.

"You're clear to pass!"

The shout broke my trance. A giant inflatable Frankenstein painted red loomed ahead. Signs were posted everywhere. I passed through Hell's Gate.

And so, I had the privilege of cycling another forty-one miles in the scorching heat of Texas. There seemed to be more medical tents than water stops. Cyclists belly-flopped into inflatable kiddie pools. Rows of cots lined under tents with IV bags laced into arms. I pushed past all of it. I kept pedaling.

I kept burning.

For those of you counting, you might wonder why I cycled another 41 miles after passing Hell's Gate, which was erected at the 61-mile mark. You'd add the two numbers for a combined total of 102 miles. You'd laugh that I couldn't count properly, which, as you know by now, is actually true. For your information, I cycled another 41 miles past Hell's Gate because the one hundred in the name Hotter'N Hell Hundred is apparently just a guidepost. Often, Triple-H is a little longer because I guess the organizers thought the cyclists would enjoy a few more miles of total dehydration and the beautiful scenery of blistered grass and silent birds huddled under the shade of dumpsters.

I was one of the last of the nine thousand that finished. I found and defeated another impossible goal. I completed a century ride in the hottest race in America, on the hottest day in its history. I had my story and my T-shirt to prove it.

Besides the bragging and testing and burning, there was one more reason I'd picked Hotter'N Hell. You see, I'd been to hell once before. The bomb had buried me into a hot, sulfur pit of death. Back then, I'd been hopeless and helpless to save myself. Now, sixteen years later, I'd ridden into hell on my own free will and climbed out with the power of hope. The moment I crossed that finish line, I was no longer a victim. I was no longer a survivor. My new name was Champion.

Part Three

SERVANT

2017 Ironman Arizona

Hour Sixteen

FOR THE FINAL thirteen miles of the marathon, my legs hurt. I didn't feel my pink flame of hope slicing through the fires. It was just pain. Cramps gripped my thighs so tightly I had to double over and knead them until the cramps passed. My legs moved like noodles and I had to intentionally exert energy from whatever muscle fibers were still intact. No mental storm overwhelmed my mind. I was fully aware of how I struggled for every breath and the sound of each athlete's steps as they passed me.

It was dark and I started getting confused. The run course doubled back three times on one side of the lake that seemed like a river before crossing over a bridge, double-backing again, sending you away from the lake for a mile loop before having to repeat the twisting and overlapping course all over again. Runners crossed in the opposite direction so often I swore they were the same five athletes. The guy with the bushy beard. The tiny girl half my age and weight. An older man with a hitch in his stride. Two power walkers with arms swinging like a military march. The guy with the bushy beard again.

I'd get to a turn or a fork and raise my arms in confusion. A purple-shirted volunteer sometimes helped. Sometimes there was no volunteer because it was approaching midnight and everyone was going home to sleep after the long day. I had to wait and massage my thighs until another athlete passed by and I'd follow. Occasionally, Erin or my husband popped out from a building or a bush. They repeated the same words, "Keep it up, you're doing great." But I saw something else in their eyes.

I was stuck in the limbo of endless loops. Time inched by and my speed kept dropping. I'd started the run at an 11-minute mile. My speed fell to a 12-minute mile. Then fourteen. Then sixteen. Then eighteen. I chugged Cokes and Red Bulls, but nothing changed. The sugar crash had come. I hadn't hit a wall. I'd fallen off the wall. And there was nothing that could put me back together again.

My mind worked hard to figure the time and the numbers. From mile markers 22 to 24, I realized that even if I doubled my speed, which would be the fastest miles I'd ever run in my entire life, I wouldn't make it. The final time cut-off was midnight and I wouldn't make it. No power of hope could change it. In just a few minutes, alone and lost in the midnight void, I would be branded with a DNF.

Chapter Nine

Drafting

THERE WAS ANOTHER reason I enjoyed cycling to work in the morning before anyone was awake. There was another motive for me to spend a full week in the summer cycling Oklahoma Freewheel and six hours every Saturday on group rides. It was the same thought I'd pondered when I took night classes for my undergraduate and my MBA, wondering why the classroom felt warmer than the couch in my own living room. After renaming myself Champion at the Hotter'N Hell Hundred, I finally decided to file for divorce.

In a divorce like mine, it was decades in the making and it didn't follow a linear path. Like many divorcees I've met, it was more like a spiral, swirling into some good seasons but back downwards into progressively worse seasons. As I've already explained, I'd set up our marriage to fail from the start. I got married wanting him to save me from myself, which was too much to ask of any man. In our first year together, I'd gained one hundred pounds and kept growing, which is probably the worst bait-and-switch marriage story I've ever heard. I'd forced the first cornerstone of our marriage to be planted on sinking sand, then I'd thrown all 355 pounds of myself into the sinking pit. And then it got worse.

I don't like to talk about our issues, even if my story might relate to others. My ex-husband is the father of my son, my most cherished blessing. My ex-husband helped me through the bad years of grief after the bombing and we had a few good seasons together after that. But no matter how hard I tried, I felt like the spiral of our relationship skewed so deep there was no visible light. Sure, maybe there was a way to save it. Maybe there would've been a miracle waiting if I'd just held on for one more year. But I know more than anyone about the problems we struggled through and I'd reached a point where I couldn't survive one week more.

Like all divorces, mine was messy and the process began long before filing and ended long after. I tried crazy, last-ditch efforts to save it, like taking a family trip to Disney World. I should have known better by then that the Disney fairy tale was a lie and there was no actual magic in the castle. My sisters and parents were shocked and unable to understand the depths of problems I'd been hiding for years. Our church friends were divided. I remember my pastor asking me in a serious conversation, "Is there another man?"

I almost spit in disgust. Not at the pastor, but for the thought. The only response I could muster was, "Why would I ever want another one of those?"

DURING THOSE MESSY YEARS, I had two more surgeries and then a third surgery after my divorce. The first one cut out my apron, which is the very accurately descriptive word for the excess skin that hung over my waist. That one surgery dropped almost thirty pounds of weight from my body. The second surgeon took care of the excess flesh around my chest and underarms. "I took care of your rocks in socks," the surgeon had said. The last surgery took out some around my waist and legs, which also muted the red scar on my shin. I drove to the mall the first day I could walk after my last surgery, my body still sore.

"Ma'am, are you sure you're alright?" the woman called for the second time outside the changing room.

"Yes," I managed to say, "just one minute more please." It would take longer than a minute to calm myself and I'd need a mop for the puddles of mascara-stained tears on the floor. For the first time in twenty years, my brain acknowledged the body in the mirror as my own.

I looked beautiful. My profile had two slight curves because my waist was smaller than my hips again. I had an actual butt instead of a flabby broadside wall. It was like I'd been blind for two decades, only hearing descriptions of sunsets or feeling the petals of a rose, and now the vivid colors of the world became real to me in a single, overwhelming moment of terrific rediscovery.

"I'm real again," I whispered through my sobs and occasionally giddy laughter.

I wasn't quite the same Amy my mind remembered. I had kept the image of the 21-year-old girl from Shreveport in my mind, refusing to accept any images of myself as I'd gained weight or, after my gastric sleeve surgery, of the wrinkled skin with stretch marks. In that dressing room, I came to terms with the 44-year-old woman. I'd given and received my share of sins, injuries, joys, struggles, love, and pain over those missing years. I had endured a total transformation in every aspect of my life. I'd gone from childless to having a son. Dangerously overweight to an attractive shape. College dropout to an MBA. Teller to Vice President. Unable to walk up a flight of steps to completing a century ride. And now: married to divorced. I felt like the world's most empowered woman. I was free to enjoy my life however I wanted. I'd reached the top of the mountain and felt there was no place higher for me to climb.

I purchased maybe seventeen outfits that day, putting it on a credit card with probably too high of an interest rate. I didn't care that day. That day I was Amy at forty-four with a real body and the scars to prove it. And I was going to celebrate, even if I celebrated alone.

But life had another surprise for me. I had one more transformation to experience. And it would come from the most surprising mentor of all.

I WAS on the front page of the Oklahoma City newspaper in January 2012. There's a close-up on my face as I'm speaking to a crowd about the third MAPS program and our mayor's weight-loss plan. The incredible success from the first and second MAPS programs fueled a drive to pass a third one, this time focused more on public spaces and infrastructure. The mayor, Mick Cornett, had invited me to his platform to speak alongside him. I'd written him an e-mail complaining about a closed bridge spanning over NW 39th Street. The closed bridge screwed up my morning bike commute to work and I challenged him on his dedication to getting Oklahoma City to lose a million pounds. With the weight and the skin surgeries, I'd lost almost two hundred pounds during his challenge and I threatened to gain it all back again if the city didn't invest in the pedestrian and cycling paths connecting the public spaces. We exchanged some e-mails and he invited me to speak at his annual State of the City Address.

Because that's the kind of community Oklahoma City shares. Anyone can engage the mayor in a conversation.

I remember feeling a sense of horror when I saw my picture in the paper. I hadn't told many people about my marriage troubles and on that day I'd decided to stop wearing my ring. In my impassioned speech about Mick's weight-loss plan, I'd put my left hand on my heart and, *snap*, the picture was taken. The front page of the newspaper had a close-up of my face and ringless hand. Some members of my family learned about my struggles from that photo and I had some explaining to do.

Looking at that picture now, I see a cold winter rage in my eyes. The painful and exhausting process of going through my upheaval at home sucked away some of my drive for issues at work. There's a term I learned later called *decision fatigue*, and it wore me out. When the mornings and evenings were spent haggling, negotiating, and side-stepping the intense emotions inside me, in my son who didn't understand our problems, and with my soon-to-be-ex-husband, there was little left in me to think about work projects. With my mental energy drained, all I had was a vast store of cold rage in my soul. The only way to calm myself was to direct my physical energy into my morning and evening workouts.

The Oklahoma City Memorial Marathon had its inaugural run in 2001, a marathon established to honor the lives of the victims and survivors of the bombing. My sister ran the full marathon in 2005, capping off her amazing transformation of losing ninety pounds with my name on her back. Our credit union had a water stop along the course and I remember thinking to myself as she passed by with a huge smile, *I wish I could do that one day*. I'd thought that was impossible since, at the time, I weighed 355 pounds. But after my weight loss and my surgeries, I knew my time had come. I decided to make my forty-fifth year of life a big one.

I signed up for the memorial marathon but that didn't seem like enough. I wanted something more than a memorial run. I wanted something to signal my new and wild freedom from the world of men. I asked around my cycling friends and we decided to schedule a special ride on my birthday, one month before the marathon. We would travel down to southwest Oklahoma near Lawton and ride through the wildlife refuge of roaming animals unhindered by fences.

I didn't know the roads down there. None of my friends did. We didn't know which roads had better blacktops, which had dangerous cracks and potholes, or where and when the traffic would hit. But the thing about the cycling community is we are all connected to almost every other cyclist in America. Every friend I asked proposed the same solution. There was a guy in Lawton who could lead the ride. I sent the guy a Facebook message and he immediately agreed. He gave me a list of options to choose from, as if he was a travel agent and had done this a hundred times before. It had taken one day to find a stranger living in a distant city to lead us.

Because that's the kind of community cyclists share.

THE CYCLING COMMUNITY was my church. The spiritual experience of burning on bikes was shared experience. We spent hours cycling hundreds of miles on country roads together. We witnessed each other at our worst selves, cursing the world on a hot summer day as we struggled to climb the final hills. That kind of experience forges a strong bond in a community, especially during Oklahoma Freewheel. In the same conversation about our children's little league games, we'd mention the color of our pee for some reassurance we weren't too dehydrated. On the bigger rides, you'd see white and pink chalk drawings on the asphalt along the way, etched by chalk angels the evening before. There were butterflies and flowers, quick encouragements and scriptures. Sometimes there were promises of donuts at the top of the hill. But the donuts were always a lie.

I never felt that deep of connection inside a church. To be fair, how could I? Even if you managed to haul the family into the car early or risked the longer lunch waiting lines to chat in the pews after the sermon, you had maybe fifteen minutes to actually talk. The rest of the time was spent in worship or listening to the preacher. After the sermon, only a small percentage of the congregation actually engaged in the act of service. Most members go to lunch and then home to watch football or their kids' baseball games or whatever else they enjoy. That doesn't make any of them bad people. That doesn't make me or my cyclist friends any more good. All I'm saying is during those two hours on Sunday mornings, it's all too easy to hide your reality and pretend you've got your world in order. I know, because I hid my marriage problems from anyone connected to our church for years.

But my cycling friends all knew the real problems because you can't hide yourself after six hours in the summer sun. We burn together, cry together, and laugh together. We listen to rock songs and sometimes even pray together amidst the buzzing of our gears. Some cyclists are atheists or agnostic, Buddhist, Hindu, Jewish, or Mormon. But we all come together and burn. We lift each other up the next hill. If one of us goes down in a crack of doom or maybe from exhaustion, the very next cyclist stops to help.

Athletes in other endurance sports share the same culture. Once, while training for a run, I was walking next to a woman in her fifties for the first time. We were trying to find the strength to start running again when she said, "Well, my husband walked in on me and my boyfriend." I choked on my own spit. She went on to explain they were going to divorce but then her husband had a heart attack. So, she stopped playing with boyfriends and stayed with her husband, helping him back to health. Now, their marriage was better than ever.

I hadn't even asked for her name yet. I found out later she was a very successful accountant and then, more than ever, I knew her random confession was only possible in the endurance community. The difference was the heavy emphasis on the word *action* in our forced inter*action*. You can only find real community when you engage in raw and real action of the mind, body, or spirit.

The reason churches with four walls exist is because, in the past, community was geography. Our towns were small enough and communication was limited to letters in the mail. The only community we had was centered around the geography of our homes. But that's not the case anymore. We have the internet and sprawling cities. Even Oklahoma City's population is an unfathomable number compared to early American history. You are just one click away from finding a community centered around whatever brings you joy, whether it's knitting or softball or cycling or gardening or camping or hiking or hunting or reading or writing or painting or singing or pottery or bird-watching or photography or running or coaching or golf or serving meals to the homeless or building wells in Africa or designing websites for nonprofits or playing video games or whatever else you could possible enjoy.

I'm not trying to discount churches. A close friend of mine is very involved in doing wonderful, giving, and charitable things as a pastor's wife. But the emphasis there is her active involvement in her church. My point isn't to leave churches. My point is, if you're in a church, do more, share more, and love more. If you are in a church where you feel disconnected, ask yourself why. If you've tried to actively engage but can't find authentic and raw relationships, then go find a new community. The real definition of church is community and, these days, community can be found anywhere. God is in all beautiful things that are shared. On Sunday mornings, He can be found inside a church and also in the drawings on country roads scratched by chalk angels.

I LEARNED one final secret of hope in those stressful years of my divorce. I spent a lot of time reflecting on my life and the major transformations I'd experienced. I'd always believed hope was something I'd done by myself, for myself. I boasted about becoming a champion on my own terms because I felt proud of my escape from victimhood and survivor-hood. But the more I re-evaluated my life, I discovered something else.

Hope thrives in community. I'm sure of that in my own life and in the countless stories I've heard from others. If you recall the four steps of hope, the last step is to take the next action on your path to your goal. That part takes courage and, more often than not, courage takes a community. By yourself, you can probably take an honest assessment, make a goal, and map a path to the goal. But finding the willpower and courage to start the next step is often too hard on our own. That's why Alcoholics Anonymous requires group sessions. It's why every successful professional athlete has a trainer or a group of trainers. Even Michael Jordan had a trainer.

In every major transformation in my life, others helped me. Sonja helped me hold on at FECU when I was about to leave. Vicky coached me into believing I was capable of being more than a clerk. Lynette revealed to me the power of hope and was by my side in my education. Donna showed me the joy of riding a bicycle, even with diaper pants. The online community in WeightWise encouraged me in my weight loss journey. And in the messy years of my marriage, in my rage, bitterness, and confusion, my cycling friends embraced me.

In cycling, it's called drafting. When you ride a bike at fifteen to twenty miles an hour, a lot of your energy is spent fighting against the wind. For every increase in your speed comes an equal increase in the wind resistance. When you ride in Oklahoma, where the wind rips car doors out of your hand, you could be pushing against an effective wind resistance of thirty to forty miles an hour. So, on group rides, we often draft. We position our bikes behind someone else, putting our front tires into the air vacuum created by their bike. It's similar to the reason birds fly in a V. The lead bird spends a lot of energy slicing the wind and the birds behind get to coast through the slip of effectively zero wind resistance.

That's how I look back at my life. In all my transformations, I drafted behind others. I borrowed their strength and courage to help me take my next step. Sometimes I did it intentionally, calling Donna for help on a school assignment or asking a cycling buddy to do an eighty-mile ride to burn away my frustrations. Other times, someone pulled ahead of me without request, like the way Vicky and Lynette led me to a distance I'd never dreamed was possible. They gave me the gift of hope when I didn't deserve it and it propelled me through my impossible transformations. My small, pink flame of hope is created by me, yes, but it is also tied to something bigger, grander, and more beautiful than myself. My hope is connected to something on the other side of evil, where hope transforms trauma and loss into empathy and love.

I know this sounds a little confusing. I don't quite understand it myself. In some ways, I believe you and only you can enact hope in your life. In other ways, I know someone else can help spark hope inside you. Those two thoughts don't seem like they can co-exist, but then again, there are lots of truths that skew away from neatly tied definitions. For example, love is something you feel for others that you and only you can choose to give or not give. But, then again, love also takes two. Joy is a feeling we experience on a deeply personal level, but joy is usually only found when that joy is shared with others.

So, even if hope can't be summed up in a perfectly rational, one-sentence definition, it's still true. To me, the slightly irrational nature of hope is precisely the reason it is beautiful, valuable, and treasured. Our inability to fully comprehend and nail down its power is the same quality of hope that transcends our minds and allows us to conquer our rational concept of the impossible.

ON THE DAY of my birthday ride in the wildlife refuge, I parked in the twilight of morning. I unhooked my bike from the rack behind my car, adjusted my tiara on my bike helmet, and slipped a pink tutu around my waist, all while badly singing, "It's my birthday and I'll be a princess if I want to."

Then Terry Head walked out of his car. He had leather-tanned skin with dark hair, dark eyes, and a Wyatt Earp mustache. The way he walked toward me made me think he was six feet tall. He seemed nothing like the pleasant man I'd pictured in our exchanged messages on Facebook. His stare was so intense my hand trembled with nervous anxiety. Or maybe excitement.

"Are you ready for this?" he asked.

I almost said *No* before quickly brushing off his question to make small talk. My friends pulled in and we hopped on our bikes to ride forty-five miles through the refuge country. Terry led the way, moving from the back of our group to the front to make sure everyone was okay and no stragglers were left behind. When we headed up a particularly challenging hill, he yelled something that sounded like the f-bomb in a heavy Scottish accent, like how William Wallace might have cursed. The surprising burst made us laugh and the hill was a little easier to climb.

"When are you going to date again?" one of my cycling friends asked me.

I repeated the same line I'd given the pastor, "Why would I ever want another one of those?" Just then, Terry whizzed past us, his thick thighs powering his bicycle at an impressive pace. "Well," I hedged, "maybe I wouldn't mind one of those."

The ride was everything I'd wanted. Near the end, I rode near Terry and discovered he had just worked a double shift. His job was to fix the critical machines on a factory floor and he hadn't slept at all the night before the ride. "Can you believe that?" I asked my girlfriends later. "He'd been awake for twenty-four hours and still led us on our 45-mile ride."

They all answered in the same way, "That's just Terry."

That kind of reputation intrigued me. Of all sexes, here was a *man* who seemed good. I hadn't encountered that level of selfless service before. After the ride, I thanked him on Facebook and he told me it was fun for him, too. I said he was lying and he again insisted. Our chats continued, moving from cycling to our lives. A couple of weeks after the ride, I was asked to speak about the bombing to a group. The talk was filling me with anxiety because we were in April and I always get anxious in April. Having to talk about the bombing meant contemplating my deceased friends and I felt the shame of surviving and the grief of loss all over again. I mentioned to Terry that I was worried I'd screw up my talk by blubbering.

It's okay, he wrote me. *The Holy Spirit will tell you what to say.*

At first, his words took me aback. Here was a cussing factory worker trying to tell me, a girl raised in church, about God. In a matter of moments, though, my confusion shifted into weeping because he was right. I wasn't practicing what I'd been taught. He barely knew me, but he was trying to spiritually lead me.

My go-to solution for my anxiety was take a long bike ride. I asked Terry to ride with me again in the wildlife refuge on April 19th, right after the morning remembrance ceremony at the Oklahoma City Memorial Museum. He agreed and, without telling anyone, I left straight from the ceremony to ride a bike with a guy I'd only met once. It was one of those days with a thin cloud cover that sharpened the colors of the world. The refuge looked more like the Irish highlands with vivid grass that seemed to emit their own light. An occasional sunray would pierce through the clouds and shine on a wild bison or maybe a small pond. I don't remember a single car passing us and I don't remember a single word Terry or I said to each other. We silently soaked in the moment, certain God had paused time and sprinkled the world with a layer of heaven.

I COMPLETED my first full Oklahoma City Memorial Marathon later that month, finally finishing the event dedicated to my fallen friends. Terry and I started to text each other and ride together more often. He started calling me by a version of my middle name, Lilly Ann. As Oklahoma Freewheel approached, I gossiped with my girlfriends about him. Surely, this was more than a cycling buddy. Buddies didn't give each other cute nicknames. They agreed and I got agitated. "Well, he better do something or nothing at all," I huffed. "I'm too old to keep guessing."

The day before the Freewheel there is a pro criterium that laps around downtown Oklahoma City. It was something of a tradition for me to have dinner downtown and watch the professional athletes on their carbon-fiber bikes race through the city streets. I asked Terry to go and we watched together. It was a warm June evening and he led me into the shade of an old church where a garden grew.

"What's that one?" he pointed to a bud with its purple petals dropping down like wet rags.

"Cone flower," I said.

"And that's a daisy, right?"

"No, that one's a coreopsis"

His walk slowed. No one was around and the wind was still. My palms started to sweat and I figured if there was ever a perfect moment to kiss, it was in a garden under the shade of a beautiful church. Terry inched toward me and my body leaned toward him. His thick mustache twitched as he parted his lips, "And what about that one?" he asked.

I stared at him. "I finally stumped you," he laughed and walked out of the garden.

He got a coffee at a street vendor and asked if I wanted something. I got a tea and the vendor asked if I wanted a lemon. I said no and the vendor asked me if I wanted sugar. I requested a Splenda. Terry paid and sat down on the concrete steps of a building. "I couldn't ask for anything more," he said as he sipped his coffee, his intense eyes focused on the professionals zipping down the street.

I'd had enough with this stupid game of dating and could hardly speak. So, I picked up my phone and sent him a text. *Are you ever going to kiss me?*

His phone lit up with the notification on the concrete step, but he didn't see it. He was still looking at the cyclists. In a moment, I realized it was the dumbest thing I'd ever done. I'd just asked a guy to kiss me in a text message. As my mind raced to figure out a way to unsend the text, I decided to knock his coffee out of his hand to spill on his phone so it would be destroyed and he'd never read my text. I'd never hang out with him again and I could go back to being an empowered woman who didn't need a man and didn't do something as juvenile as texting a guy for a kiss.

Right before I swatted at his coffee, he picked up his phone and read the text message slowly, maybe three times, to my absolute horror. I didn't breathe. "Lilly Ann," he said, finally turning his gaze toward me, "why would you want me to kiss you?"

That was it. I imagined murdering him on the spot, then decided it was better to just leave. I was so ashamed and embarrassed. He thought we were friends and I hated him for fooling me. I grabbed my keys from the step but he caught my wrist. I tried to jerk away but he leaned forward and planted a kiss on my trembling lips. My whole soul was enveloped by his scratchy mustache. It felt like my first kiss and my last kiss, and like every kiss of every movie of every romance from the beginning of time.

At forty-five years old, I finally felt the warm connection of invigorating passion and comforting strength. Something inside my soul cracked and shattered, like an ice cube thrown on hot pavement. Here, in the arms of a spandex cowboy, was my prince. As it turns out, the Disney fairy tale of true love was true. Almost. I just had to save myself, first.

One year later at the same race, Terry took me downtown to watch the cyclists. As we walked near the church where he failed to kiss me, my phone dinged. It was a text from Terry: *Will you marry me?* When I looked up from my phone, he was on his knee. I didn't hesitate. I said yes.

WE GOT MARRIED on a Saturday morning riding our bikes downtown. One of my nephews, the same little hellion that had screamed "Whoosh!" all those years ago, led the procession of my family and friends with his iPhone taped to a megaphone blasting *Chapel of Love*. I wore a white dress cut off at my thighs. Terry wore his diaper pants and a bow tie. My son, Austin, was the ring bearer. We had our vows in the garden of the church and then rode to Schlegel's Bicycles on the north edge of downtown for mimosas and muffins.

The streets of Oklahoma City were very different than when I'd first arrived. It was no longer a concrete wasteland. There were local restaurants and small retail shops. Condos were in construction and young professionals jogged with their dogs or walked to a lazy brunch. Posters advertised concerts and theater productions.

In 2014, thirty years after the '80s bust had decimated our city into a concrete wasteland, oil prices plummeted again. Oklahoma City held its breath and, to everyone's surprise, the city kept growing. Historical buildings continued to be renovated. Companies continued to move their national headquarters to our city. Young couples and families flourished in Oklahoma City neighborhoods and labeled themselves *The MAPS Generation.*

The Thunder never won a championship, but we didn't need it anymore. The transformation had worked. Outside Oklahoma City, many don't remember the bombing. Part of that is the passage of time. But a great part is the work the city did for itself. Mayor Mick Cornett, who announced the completion of the city's million pounds lost, was asked to speak around the country to explain our seemingly impossible transformation. People across the country asked the same question, "How could this happen in a place like Oklahoma City?"

And we aren't done yet.

As I've experienced, hope never stops. Once you've built a culture of hope, the wildfire continues to burn. Like other cities, we still have our share of problems. Big problems. We have a homeless problem. An incarceration problem. A racial disparity problem. An education problem. A gambling problem. A meth problem. The list goes on and on. But, with the power of hope, we have plans to tackle all of them. If you ask your average citizen in Oklahoma City, they will beam with confidence that we can fix our problems. Not somebody else. Not some national task force. Our community, and our community alone, has the power to change.

In December of 2019, Oklahoma City passed the fourth MAPS program. This one dedicated almost one *billion* dollars to building a massive living quarters for the homeless, providing assistance to the mentally ill, constructing new pedestrian walkways and bike paths, and beautifying long-forgotten segments of the city that had been decimated from old rules of redlining and racial prejudices. The new tax passed with over seventy percent approval, celebrated by a MAPS generation born and bred in a city that has proven, over and over, that impossible transformation is possible, after all.

When I packed up my life in Shreveport, I had imagined Oklahoma City as a shining city on a hill. I'd called it a city of hope because I didn't understand what the word *hope* meant. I was thinking it was a city of fantasy, a city that would magically make my every dream come true. Now that I understand hope's true meaning, I believe the label was right. Oklahoma City shines on the hill because it's a city on fire. We continue to burn in our transformations to become something better, our eyes aimed at a brighter future. If you can call us anything, we are a city of hope.

AFTER MY WEDDING, Allegiance had one of our annual meetings. Lynette got on stage to recognize some of the longevity milestones of our employees. She handed our CFO, Sabrina, her recognition and, in an off-hand comment, said, "If anything happened to me, Sabrina would be the one to keep us afloat."

At home, I stomped around in a fuss, talking out loud more to myself than to Terry. "After everything we've been through, she's going to say that. She's the one that made me do the painted picture to begin with. She knows this is the job I've been working toward."

After I calmed down with a glass of wine, I sat on the couch and curled into Terry's arms. "I don't think she meant Sabrina would be CEO," Terry said softly. "But even if she did, why would that matter?"

"Because I'm the one that's supposed to be CEO. That's my goal."

"But why do you want it?"

I thought for a long minute and was surprised that I didn't have an answer.

Terry lifted my chin. "You could work as a cashier at the Piggly Wiggly and we'd still be full of joy."

Over the next week, I thought about his words. He was right. I didn't need the title anymore. I wasn't sure why I'd ever wanted it. Maybe I'd wanted the fame or prestige. Maybe I had been carrying the shame of being a bad teller and Vicky's last pick. Or maybe it was the guilt of surviving. Whatever the reason I wrote those three letters on my painted picture, it was gone now. I didn't need the title to feel empowered, strong, or joyful. A corner office wouldn't change my rich friendships in my cycling community. The deep wound of my loneliness staring into the dark void in Shreveport had been fully healed with Terry's love. I had a supreme peace following his lead. Nothing brought me more joy than sitting next to him on the curb of a rundown convenience store, enjoying a bag of salty chips and a real

Coke after a long bike ride.

"You're right," I told him a week later. "We just need each other and our bikes . . . and maybe wi-fi."

2017 Ironman Arizona

Hour Seventeen

IT WAS FIVE minutes to midnight and I was still a mile away from the finish. A golf cart came into view with two kids, maybe in their twenties, waving in my direction. I was stumbling forward but I knew it was over. I couldn't finish the last mile in five minutes. These two kids were going to take my chip and brand me with a DNF. Here, with one mile left in my impossible race, I'd failed.

"God," I whispered as I considered running around the golf cart. "If there's any way to finish, I can't do it. You'll have to finish for me."

"Amy!" Erin ran onto the running path. "You can make it."

"It's midnight," I said as the golf cart pulled up to us.

"When the cannon fired, where were you?" Erin asked me, ignoring the kids trying to interrupt us.

My brain was in a fog. *What did the cannon have to do with midnight?* "I was at the lake."

"Waiting in line, right?"

"Yeah."

"Amy," she patted my back, "you got in the lake fifteen minutes after the canon blast. So, you still have fifteen minutes to finish."

She was right. In my daze of dehydration and exhaustion, I'd forgotten that part. Every athlete had seventeen hours to finish from the moment they jumped in the lake. I'd jumped in fifteen minutes *after* the cannon blast. So, I could still complete the race if I passed the finish line by 12:15 a.m. I didn't have five minutes. I had twenty.

"Wait, what?" one of the kids in the cart asked.

"Athlete," Erin said, "you're going to make it. But you have to hustle. Now!"

Something ignited in my soul and I ran. My sight blurred but my pink flame of hope lit my path through my pain. As I ran, I was aware the flame wasn't my own. I had no strength left. Instead, my hope surged with a power from somewhere else.

The memories of my mentors encircled me and tossed branches of their wisdom into my flame. I felt Sonja's laugh and Vicky's love. Lynette's speech of trimming the fat and her purple chairs. Donna's encouragement that sometimes you have to jump first and build your wings on the way down. My dad winked. Ruth smiled from the finish line. My surgeon reminded me that we have only a brief window of time to change our life. Terry leaned into my fire and whispered, "You are my champion."

I threw my soul into the fire and every desire in my life was consumed. Only one thing drew me toward the finish. It felt like an anointing. It was a responsibility that, somehow, made me soar. It was the crystal-clear thought that I would cross the finish line for them. For my sisters. For my parents. For my friends. For my son in Oklahoma trying to get accepted into a university. For my co-workers who felt trapped in life and couldn't see a path to change. I ran to prove to others that impossible was a lie. Impossible was the fantasy we dreamed in our mind. I ran to show the pink flame of hope was real. I burned in the final mile because hope is a verb that makes all things possible.

The darkness gave way to floodlights. I ran into the finish-line chute as time ticked away. A roar from the stands rose to match the raging fire inside me. With all my mentors pushing me, I shot across the final line with my arms held high.

"AMY DOWNS," Mike's voice boomed in the electric air as I collapsed into Terry's laughing chest. "YOU ARE AN IRONMAN!"

Chapter Ten

Soaring

TWO MONTHS AFTER becoming an Ironman, I was named the CEO of Allegiance. This time, I had a renewed focus on the reason why, inspired by Terry when he came home from a twelve-hour shift on the factory floor with slumped shoulders and bright eyes. "Man," he'd smile, "me and the boys went balls-to-the-wall today." They'd repaired machines and avoided big disasters, circling each other all day to keep the factory running. Their camaraderie reminded me of why I wanted to lead our credit union. I didn't want the title. I wanted to serve.

I had such a long and deep history with Allegiance, I felt no one could serve our employees or our members better. No one else could propel our culture of empowerment and service better. Just like Vicky and Lynette had done for me, I wanted to reach down and pull others out of whatever hopeless prison they suffered. It was time to repay all the hope I'd borrowed.

But there was one big problem. Lynette's strength was in accounting. Sabrina, our CFO, was an accounting wizard. I may have passed my math classes to get my MBA, but I knew it was a weak spot for me. Lynette knew it. Sabrina knew it. Our board knew it. I enrolled in online classes to try to learn more, but no matter how many classes

I tried, I struggled.

"I can't be like you," I confessed in Sabrina's office. She looked up from her computer in surprise. "You will always be smarter and more experienced with our numbers. I know the board wants to see that in our next CEO, but I can't do it." Sabrina stared at me without a word. What could she say? She and I had never spoken about who would replace Lynette, but we both knew Sabrina was an option.

Then I asked a crazy question. "Would you help me better understand some of this stuff?"

I saw Sabrina calculate. She could have answered with anything. She could have been too busy to work with me. She could have promised to schedule some time next week and then forgotten. She could have just told me no, there was no way for her to explain it to me. But she said none of those things. Instead, she smiled. "I'd love to," she said and pulled some spreadsheets up on her screen to start teaching.

That story sounds odd if you live in the normal corporate world. You'd never see a woman dedicate hours every week to ensure someone else got a position she was qualified to fill. But if you live in the credit union world, it happens all the time. We live by our motto. Our core culture makes serving others our default, even if it's at our own expense. It's the core of our not-for-profit business model. It's in the heart of our volunteer board members, who aren't paid. It's the reason Tinker Federal Credit Union and others across the country spent time and resources to save our credit union, with no compensation or publicity. We are dedicated to a higher purpose than profit or gain.

With Sabrina's help, I finally understood some of the finer nuances of credit union finance. Lynette and the board were impressed with my progress and, in the end, they chose me to be the next CEO. But by then, I would have loved to serve Sabrina if she'd been chosen instead. That's the thing about servant leadership. When you receive it, you're willing to give it back tenfold. It's the secret strength of the credit union mantra: "People helping people."

HOPE MEANS NOTHING without a purpose, and that purpose must be for a better tomorrow. Better doesn't mean a title. It's not a bank account. It's not a home or a facelift or a six pack or a child pitching a perfect game in little league. Better is a virtue. Better is empowerment and freedom from a prison of your own making. Sometimes that involves a title, or money, or a nip and tuck here or there, but those should never be the goal. If they are, then you're in for a future that is worse. You're signing up for a future where there is never enough to satisfy. A life with no sustaining peace, love, or joy. Above all other goals you could write on an index card, service is the highest. The only reason to soar is to help lift someone else from the ground.

There are lots of self-motivation and inspiration books in the market. I've learned a lot from the wise words in many of them. But some books miss the point. They encourage you to get up, move, change and charge so you can be better than anyone else around. If that speaks to you, go for it. I'll be in the stands cheering the loudest as you cross the finish line. Just remember that's not the end of your life. There's something far greater and lovelier than success.

The beautiful gift of hope I'd received over my years changed me. It filled me so full that I felt like hope spewed from my fingers and lips. In this short life that can end at any moment, I feel almost rushed to give more back. Every time I can share some of the lessons I was taught, an almost unbearable joy sets me ablaze. It is a better and more fulfilling experience than walking the stage to receive my MBA, losing one hundred pounds, being an Ironman, or handing out my business card with the title CEO.

I never expected it, but the greatest joy in hope is giving it to someone else.

SONJA'S DAUGHTER came to work at Allegiance. Her name is Savanna and I threw her baby shower while she was still in Sonja's womb. Savanna looks so much like her mom that I often stared at her on the teller line, the old memories of my old friend bubbling emotions inside me. It felt good to have Savanna at Allegiance. She made it feel more like home for me with her mom's hilarious attitude. We made quick friends and texted often. Once, I gave her a card written in only emojis.

She had grown up being very close to her sister. Their dad had remarried, but they always missed their mom. One April, when my anxiety peaked near the bombing anniversary, I confided in Savanna how guilty I felt to have lived. Her mom had died leaving two daughters and, at the time, I didn't have any kids. Savanna looked at me, confused, and almost shouted, "Amy, we thank God you survived."

Savanna didn't want to work at a credit union. She wanted to work at the FBI, which made sense given how the bombing impacted her life. She'd applied multiple times to the FBI but they hadn't offered her a position yet. She had tried, but had come up short. Just like Lynette had done for me, I walked Savanna through the steps of hope. I explained she needed to make a new path to the FBI because there is *always* hope.

Oklahoma had just passed a medical marijuana law and banking cash from a controlled substance took a lot of work. Most financial institutions, ours included, wouldn't touch cash from the industry because of the highly detailed and labor-intensive reporting it required. But there was one local bank that was accepting deposits. I made some calls for more information and told Savanna about the opportunity. If the FBI wouldn't take her right now, then she needed to get more unique experiences that related to their work. Illegal drug reporting and banking sounded like something that would impress the FBI. Savanna applied to the bank and, standing on her own resume and experience at Allegiance, she got the job.

On my way home after Savanna's last day, I prayed in my car, "She'll be fine, Sonja. Just like you were, she's stronger than me."

LAST AUGUST, I pulled some weeds out of my garden in the heat of the Oklahoma summer sun. "Time to hit the road," Terry called from our back door. The University of Oklahoma was playing a home football game and Austin was in the marching band. We had to be there a few hours early because I liked to watch him roam Campus Corner performing with his drumline on the streets. I didn't like to attend the actual games. That large crowd with explosive guns and fireworks sometimes sent my mind into another anxiety attack.

I clutched a fistful of the fertilized soil and thought of my friends. The bomb had been constructed with a kind of fertilizer. The same instrument of terrible destruction could also produce the beautiful and diverse colors of tiger lilies, Mexican yarrow, and pink azaleas. The thought reminded me of something I'd recently discovered. The words from my mother's lullaby are found in the same Psalm I quoted while buried under the rubble. The same song that laments our walks through the valleys of the shadow of death finishes with the promise of goodness and mercy to follow all the days of our lives.

My favorite flower rises high in the center of my garden. The Sonja sunflowers may look like the sun, but that's not why sunflowers get their name. The most interesting behavior of sunflowers is they move throughout the day, twisting their stems and broad yellow bulbs to face directly into the sun as it arcs across the sky, basking and thriving in the fierce heat.

As if to praise the fire that burns.

Acknowledgements

THIS BOOK has been in development for nearly a decade. I kept struggling with my overall message even with the help of some brilliant and gifted agents, collaborators, and writers. With every attempt, I couldn't seem to bridge the lessons from both my survival and success into a single message.

I spent time in prayer, reflected over my twenty years of speeches, and re-read the old and various rough draft versions of this book. The word I kept coming back to was hope. Crazy hope, wild hope, bright hope, active hope, and sustaining hope. A friend and collaborator suggested that I read a recently published book called *Hope Rising: How the Science of Hope Can Change Your Life*.

It was like the two authors, Casey Gwinn and Chan Hellman, were writing about my life. Their description of hope drawn from decades of scientific research and in-depth case studies matched with every speech I'd ever given. From my clarity while buried, to Lynette's magic wand, to the old adage about swallowing an elephant, their lives' work proved those concepts are critical steps to enacting hope in anyone's life. I instantly knew they were right because I experienced the path of hope they described decades before they published their book. They summed up the transformative and active power of hope by writing the words: *hope is a verb*. Using their blueprints for hope, I was finally able to see the bridge connecting my life's journey from survivor to champion and beyond. If you doubt anything I've said, please check out *Hope Rising*, I guarantee you'll be convinced hope is a verb you can enact today to transform your life into the future of your dreams.

There's a long list of people who made this book possible. For starters, all those mentioned in the book had such a positive impact on my life and cannot be thanked enough.

My life wouldn't have been the same without the incredible leadership I received from Lynette.

I am thankful to all the employees and volunteers of Federal Employees Credit Union/Allegiance Credit Union, both past and present, for the friendships, memories, and growth opportunities over the last 32 years. I am thankful for my surviving co-workers Terri, Bobbi, and Lisa who still work there today and are able to reassure me each April that I am feeling is normal. I will never forget our 18 co-workers at Federal Employees Credit Union who were killed on April 19, 1995:

Kimberly Ruth Burgess, 29, Oklahoma City
Kathy A. Finley, 44, Yukon
Jamie (Fialkowski) Genzer, 32, Wellston
Linda Coleen Housley, 53, Oklahoma City
Robbin Ann Huff, 37, Bethany
Christi Yolanda Jenkins, 32, Edmond
Valerie Jo Koelsch, 33, Oklahoma City
Kathy Cagle Leinen, 47, Oklahoma City
Claudette (Duke) Meek, 43, Oklahoma City
Frankie Ann Merrell, 23, Oklahoma City
Jill Diane Randolph, 27, Oklahoma City
Claudine Ritter, 48, Oklahoma City
Christy Rosas, 22, Moore
Sonja Lynn Sanders, 27, Moore
Karan Howell Shepherd, 27, Moore
Victoria Jeanette Texter, 37, Oklahoma City
Virginia M. Thompson, 56, El Reno
Tresia Jo "Mathes" Worton, 28, Oklahoma City

I owe so much to my friend and author Martha Fouts, who helped and encouraged me to find my message.

I am so grateful for the people who agreed to read the rough draft of the final version and offer feedback. Thank you Jim Hargrove, Lance Haffner, John Cooper, Brent Rempe, Caroline Willard, Mike

Kloiber, Brad Bishop, Alysha Welliver, Julie Dill, Farrah Snow, and Renee Ward, as well as our grammatical editor Adam Palmer.

The bold and beautiful book design was a concept from a 99designs.com contest that was finely tuned by the very skilled Matthew Henderson. Thanks to Matt Ward for patiently working with me to record my Audible version. And a special thanks to David Skidmore for helping me generate new and exciting ideas on presenting this message in my speeches.

Of course, I owe much to every member of my family who helped raise and encourage me on my journey.

And how do I properly thank my nephew, Caleb McCoy? He dedicated over a year of his life to work on my book without any promise of payment, in addition to grinding through his full-time job and juggling his family, all because he believed my story needed to be told. In the writing world Caleb is called my "ghost writer" but he isn't a ghost and I am proud to tell everyone about his writing. Caleb spent hours with me every weekend pulling out the stories and memories from the corners of my mind. He organized the flow of the story in such a creative way. He worked on the book each morning before leaving for his office to work as an attorney during the day. He wrote and revised several iterations of the book before we got to our final version. He stood up to an agent who tried to turn the story into something that wasn't true and was willing to risk no compensation in order to stay true to my message. Caleb would say that he shouldn't fall in love with his own work in order to be a good writer. Well, he might not be in love with his work, but I sure am! I can never thank him enough for all he has done.

Finally, and most importantly I want to acknowledge everyone else not mentioned who was involved in the events and aftermath of April 19, 1995. Nothing I could say in this book or in the acknowledgements could convey the beautiful lives, selfless sacrifices, or tragic deaths. There is nothing I could ever do to repay the brave firefighters of Station Eight who risked their lives to save mine. I hope you will take some time learn more about the legacy of that day and help support the preservation and advocacy efforts of the Oklahoma City National Memorial Museum by visiting www.memorialmuseum.com.

Made in the USA
Middletown, DE
28 April 2020

92292694R10111